brilliant

social media

PEARSON

At Pearson, we believe in learning – all kinds of learning for all kinds of people. Whether it's at home, in the classroom or in the workplace, learning is the key to improving our life chances.

That's why we're working with leading authors to bring you the latest thinking and the best practices, so you can get better at the things that are important to you. You can learn on the page or on the move, and with content that's always crafted to help you understand quickly and apply what you've learned.

If you want to upgrade your personal skills or accelerate your career, become a more effective leader or more powerful communicator, discover new opportunities or simply find more inspiration, we can help you make progress in your work and life.

Pearson is the world's leading learning company. Our portfolio includes the Financial Times, Penguin, Dorling Kindersley, and our educational business, Pearson International.

Every day our work helps learning flourish, and wherever learning flourishes, so do people.

To learn more please visit us at: **www.pearson.com/uk**

brilliant

social media

How to start, refine and improve your social media business strategy

Adam Gray

PEARSON

Harlow, England • London • New York • Boston • San Francisco • Toronto • Sydney • Auckland • Singapore • Hong Kong
Tokyo • Seoul • Taipei • New Delhi • Cape Town • São Paulo • Mexico City • Madrid • Amsterdam • Munich • Paris • Milan

PEARSON EDUCATION LIMITED

Edinburgh Gate
Harlow CM20 2JE
United Kingdom
Tel: +44 (0)1279 623623
Web: www.pearson.com/uk

First published 2013 (print and electronic)

© Pearson Education Limited 2013 (print and electronic)

The right of Adam Gray to be identified as author of this work has been asserted by him in accordance with the Copyright, Designs and Patents Act 1988.

Pearson Education is not responsible for the content of third-party internet sites.

ISBN: 978-1-292-00113-5 (print)
        978-1-292-00114-2 (PDF)
        978-1-292-00115-9 (ePub)
        978-1-292-00603-1 (eText)

British Library Cataloguing-in-Publication Data
A catalog record for the print edition is available from the British Library

Library of Congress Cataloging-in-Publication Data
Gray, Adam (Business writer)
  Brilliant social media : how to start, refine and improve your social media business strategy / Adam Gray.
    pages cm
  Includes index.
  ISBN 978-1-292-00113-5 (pbk.) -- ISBN 978-1-292-00114-2 (PDF) -- ISBN 978-1-292-00115-9 (ePub) -- ISBN 978-1-292-00603-1 (eText)
  1. Internet marketing. 2. Social media--Economic aspects. 3. Online social networks. I. Title.
  HF5415.1265.G738 2013
  658.8'72--dc23
                                    2013027160

10 9 8 7 6 5 4 3 2 1
17 16 15 14 13

Print edition typeset in Plantin 10/14pt by 30
Print edition printed and bound in Great Britain by Ashford Colour Press Ltd, Gosport, Hampshire

NOTE THAT ANY PAGE CROSS-REFERENCES REFER TO THE PRINT EDITION

Contents

Publisher's acknowledgements

We are grateful to the following for permission to reproduce copyright material:

Figures

Figure 6.1 adapted from The Conversation Prism, www.theconversationprism.com, © Brian Solis, www.briansolis.com and JESS3; Figure 7.1 from LinkedIn; Figure 14.1 from bitly with permission from bitly.com; Figures 14.2, 14.3, 14.4 from http://sproutsocial.com, Sprout Social; Figure 19.1 from Fab.com, owner of the website content (excluding photo) is Fab.com, Inc., photo with permission from Design House Stockholm.

In some instances we have been unable to trace the owners of copyright material, and we would appreciate any information that would enable us to do so.

About the author

Adam has spent 25 years in marketing, working for agencies and clients in the UK, Europe, Russia and Africa. He began marketing in the days before email, then moved into digital marketing, and was even working on some of the very earliest social networks. Then, about five years ago, frustrated by what he believed to be the failings of traditional marketing channels and techniques, he made the decision to work exclusively in social media.

Now he consults with medium and large companies (and some interesting small ones), helping them to gain traction in and avoid the dangers of operating in the social media world. He writes articles for a wide range of publications and speaks to businesses and in education as a guest lecturer at several business-focused universities. He also speaks for the Chartered Institute of Marketing, the Institute of Sales and Marketing Management and the Chartered Institute of Professional Development about the impact of social media on business and society.

You can, not surprisingly, find Adam all over the world of social media: on Twitter he's @TheAdamGray and @AGSocialMedia, on LinkedIn he's AdamGray and on Facebook he's AdamGraySocialMedia. Then, of course, at www.GrayUK.com you can follow his blog and download various resources and guides.

About the book (go on, read me)

Generally, I'm not a fan of business books. Usually, the problem is that they're not very well written and consequently I find them really difficult to read. So I have tried very hard to make this book an exception by distilling what I know into the most logical and helpful order.

I also find that many business books assume I am an idiot. They take a concept and then describe why it is so from 50 different directions, stating and restating the same point over and over again. I will explain concepts, but I won't do it repeatedly. There's a glossary at the end of the book, which might help with some of the names of things.

Finally, I didn't want to spend the whole book justifying the existence of social media and trying to 'sell' the belief that it is a good thing. I am a social media evangelist. I think it is a good thing and I believe that history will look back on Mark Zuckerberg, Reid Hoffman and Biz Stone (among others) as having achieved more than most from this era.

Social media isn't just about making money and discovering/storing information about you. In fact, Facebook's mission statement is, 'To make the world a more open and connected place'. Yes, Facebook* now makes lots of money from selling advertising based on the insight that this information gives them about you and me, but that's the nature of the modern world – organisations store data about us and they use this data to try and sell us stuff based on what we've said we do and like. The difference is that these new social companies have learned to harness this most effectively for their businesses and you need to do the same.

All of the statements I've made in this book are based on the fact that 'we are where we are'. There's no use in debating whether engaging on Facebook* is morally right or wrong or if Facebook will even be around in another decade (look how quickly MySpace went from being the biggest site on the internet to almost nothing). Facebook is here and strong for the moment and it is a major part of how modern people spend their time and engage with their friends.

Social media is here. That may sound like I'm stating the obvious, but we all need to acknowledge that social media is part of the modern world and for many people it is one of the ways they choose to do research and to forge relationships, not necessarily the only way or even the most important way, but one of the ways nonetheless.

These days it is important for a business to have an effective and active presence on social media, just like it is important for them to have a website and email. People expect to be able to find businesses everywhere they look and a failure to have a social presence increasingly begs the question, 'Why not? Why don't they want to talk to their customers?'

So, with this book I will guide you through the thinking behind social media and will provide a step-by-step guide to setting up, running and improving/refining all of the necessary accounts that you will need if you are going to be really successful in the social media space.

As I started to write this book I realised that what I wanted to do was to strike a balance between assuming a level of knowledge

---

* In this section when I say Facebook I use this to mean Facebook/LinkedIn/Twitter/Google+ and any one of the major social platforms.

that perhaps you don't yet have and covering ground that you already know. So I have made some assumptions about your level of understanding about marketing, digital marketing and social media. I will try each time I introduce a new topic to mention the points that you need to understand before I plunge straight in.

There will be further information available on my website (**www. GrayUK.com/brilliant**), which you can visit to see some interactive content and some more detailed discussion on some of the topics we cover here.

This isn't a visual guide to using any of the platforms I mention, partly because by the time this book is published, something will have changed, but also because I don't want to needlessly replicate information that these platforms already provide. If you want more technical help on setting up an account or on a particular function, I strongly recommend looking at the site's help pages. They're often extremely useful and will probably provide the answer.

By the end of this book I hope that you will:

- understand the way the social media world operates
- discover how social media can overcome business issues that traditional marketing can't
- plan and implement a social media strategy
- identify opportunities to use social media to gain a competitive advantage
- feel empowered enough to go out into the social media world and stake your claim!

If you're feeling that social media sounds difficult, or too much like a full-time job, then don't. The reality of social media and its use in business and personal life is that it's really easy. You might very well be doubting that, given we're just at the beginning of this book, but the basic dynamics of what goes on in social media are easy to grasp. The way that news and information spread and relationships are built is exactly the same as the way in which these things happen in the real world, so if you give it a try and invest a little bit of time and effort, you and your business will be just fine.

Introduction: embracing change

At heart I am a late adopter, a Luddite if you like. I'm not actually scared of technology and change, but I am at best a little wary of it. However, over the years I've learned to accept and embrace it. I've learned that new technology is a good thing – it enables change, and change is good.

Over the last decade I have seen a revolution in how we communicate. The advent of broadband, 3G and high-powered technology has seen the rise of an always-on internet and email-powered life. These changes have been every bit as important and far-reaching as the printing press, radio and television, but the difference is that these changes have happened in a few years rather than decades.

Social media has been around for only a decade, and in just a short amount of time the way we communicate has changed profoundly. What began as a few developers and enthusiasts in the UK and the US has become a global phenomenon that has enabled friends to keep in touch with each other and talk about the things which matter to them. Perhaps more importantly, though, we have changed our behaviours. Now, checking Facebook, Twitter and LinkedIn is as ingrained in our daily lives as shaking hands and eating lunch.

In October 2012 Facebook passed the milestone of *1 billion* members. Let's put that in perspective: only India and China have a greater population than Facebook and it's more than the entire population of the world in 1800. And it's not just about Facebook – of the top ten most populous places to be, five of them are countries (China, India, the US, Indonesia and Brazil) and five are social media platforms (Facebook, Twitter, YouTube, LinkedIn, Google+). This just goes to show you how important these platforms are to people, so why wouldn't you want to use them for your business?

It's not just that these sites are popular – when you realise how essential they've become, it's even more imperative to join up. Over half of the adult UK population is on Facebook; 80 per cent of senior roles in the US are now filled via LinkedIn. Many news stories are 'broken' on Twitter. More people meet their life partners online than those who meet in bars, clubs and social gatherings combined. Even political regimes are overthrown by crowds mobilised by using the free tools that are social media. We've seen unimaginable changes in places such as Egypt, Africa and the Middle East, all of which have been enabled by social media.

Social media is now a part of everyday life. Failure to acknowledge, join and use these networks isn't going to mean that you have no opportunities for your business tomorrow, but it will make life much more difficult in the future.

I'm writing this book from a place of having been a digital sceptic for a decade in marketing and an advocate and champion for another decade. I've worked with small and large companies, given presentations and taught courses, so whatever you need help with I've probably already been asked that question. All of the suggestions and recommendations I make in this book are based on my practical experience of things that really work, rather than things I have just read about.

I hope that this book will help you realise what social media can do for you and your business, so you can embrace the future in a positive and fresh way.

Welcome to *Brilliant Social Media*.

CHAPTER 1

Setting the scene – how marketing used to work

J effrey Cruikshank is generally credited with having invented modern marketing in the early 1900s. Over the next couple of decades this was refined by some of the best-known names in advertising, many of whom live on as the names of large agencies such as Leo Burnett, David Ogilvy and J. Walter Thompson. They all discovered that showing a message to people when they weren't expecting it was a surprisingly effective tool in changing people's behaviour to get them to buy a product.

This technique became known as 'interruption marketing', because you quite literally interrupted people – naturally. Ever since then marketing has largely been based on the idea of interrupting people with your message.

Typically, we advertise (all over the place), we use direct mail, we use sponsorship, events, sampling, partnerships … in fact, we use every imaginable way of getting our brand and our message in front of unsuspecting customers in the hope that at some point they will say, 'Yes, that's it, I need to buy your product'.

Marketing campaigns use a variety of channels to interrupt people and marketing departments have at their disposal a huge number of tools to try to do this, including, among many:

- *advertising*: TV, radio, print (newspapers, magazines, etc.), directories, online (banner ads), pay per click (PPC) (such as Google's AdWords, Facebook, LinkedIn), outdoor (posters, supersites, bus shelters, etc.) and other (taxis, buses, floor stickers, shopping trolleys)

- *direct communication*: direct mail (leaflets, letters, etc.), email marketing
- *sponsorship*: logos (on shirts, racing cars, etc.), TV programme sponsorship (*Coronation Street* is brought to you by ...), event sponsorship (the Gillette London Marathon, etc.)
- *events*: exhibitions, seminars, hospitality
- *search*: being found on Google/Bing/Yahoo!

Most of these marketing techniques are not in themselves a response mechanism (by which I mean that they don't allow for a dialogue, only a monologue). They do, however, act as a signpost to point prospects towards a central point. These days, for most organisations marketing really means 'digital marketing' and all of the different tools listed above are used for the purpose of driving as much traffic as possible to the website where you can present your messages to people.

> for most organisations marketing really means 'digital marketing'

 brilliant definition

Digital marketing is the use of electronic/digital channels such as website, email, social media and PPC advertising to spread your message, raise awareness and hopefully increase sales.

Your website is, and probably always will be, the central point of your digital marketing presence. On your website, unlike anywhere else, you can create a look and feel that is exactly as you want it to be. The colours, size, interaction and functionality are all totally within your control, which isn't possible on the various social platforms (although a degree of personalisation is available on all of them).

The expectation is that people will arrive at your website, browse, learn about your business and then, with luck, will email/telephone/buy. It really is as easy as that – or is it?

The question is, should you really be basing your digital marketing, and therefore your marketing, and therefore the development of your business, on luck? (You probably didn't even notice that I used the expression 'with luck' in the last paragraph.)

If you have the Google Analytics (or similar) web statistics tool installed on your website you can get all sorts of insights into how many visitors you attract and what they do when they're there. Typically, you may get an average number of page views of perhaps three or so per visitor – that is, how many pages of your website they've looked at during their visit. I'd be surprised if it's many more than this unless you're Amazon. So, during this average number of pages per visit, has the visitor learned enough about you to make the decision about whether or not you are the right person to be delivering the product or service they want? Probably not.

> you can get all sorts of insights into how many visitors you attract

The problem with basing your marketing strategy on simply driving visitors to your website is that it presupposes they care. The truth is that they probably don't. The reason that you can't expect them to spend ages browsing around is people who have searched, clicked, read an ad or seen a logo on a car usually arrive at your website not knowing you from Adam (if you'll excuse the pun) and you've not yet earned the right to expect them to invest time with you. All they have to make a decision on whether or not to invest that time (or money) with you is if they like/appreciate/connect with your website, based on the design (subjective), the wording (subjective), the colours (subjective) … you get the idea. It's not looking great.

Aside from the problem of websites, there's another bigger issue to deal with. Traditional thinking and marketing are no longer producing the same kinds of results that they used to. In fact, response rates are falling across the board. So what's changed since 'the good old days'? Well, there are probably four main issues.

- *Inundation – everybody's doing it.* It doesn't matter whether we're talking about direct mail, email marketing, advertising, sponsorship, inserts in magazines … there are loads of companies doing the same thing as you. Loads of companies vying for our attention. You need only look at how many inserts are included in the next magazine that you buy or what percentage of your post is junk mail you didn't ask for from companies trying to sell to you or how full your spam folder gets on your computer. Because of this explosion of 'stuff' we are exposed to, very little of it catches our eye in the way that it used to. We've become extremely adept at 'sifting' the veritable tsunami of communications we receive through all channels, so we only engage with the stuff that interests us.

- *Fragmentation – there's just so much choice.* When I was a child there was just one commercial TV channel. When I was a teenager there were two commercial TV channels. Now there are 400 commercial channels. Also, it isn't just TV channels – there are tens of thousands of magazine titles and I am subjected to ads everywhere I look, from the handle of my shopping trolley to the back of the bus I'm stuck behind in traffic. This makes the job of any marketer looking to target me with their message very difficult, as I could be in any one of a hundred places and it's impossible to place adverts everywhere.

- *Empowerment – the visitors are in control.* Once upon a time people believed what they read in advertisements, but research now shows that fewer than 20 per cent of consumers trust advertisements. The internet means it is now far easier to discover 'the truth' and people are in a position to check the

> people are in a position to check the validity of claims and facts instantly

validity of claims and facts instantly. Perhaps more worryingly, when they search for a product or service (including yours), literally hundreds of other possible suppliers are only a click or two away.

- *Everybody's good – or so they claim.* Everybody offers 'outstanding customer service', 'exceptional value for money', 'satisfaction guaranteed' … and because everyone's saying it, there's no longer any differentiation.

In short, marketing as we knew it doesn't work any more. Because of this we are seeing media companies struggling to fill advertising space, so are giving it away. We even see TV adverts advertising TV adverts on TV!

brilliant tip

With all your competitors online and selling a similar product or service to you, try to make yourself look different. Talk about what you do in a different way, offer a unique service or describe what you do in an unusual way.

What your marketing needs is for your audience to arrive at your website having already built a relationship with you, already loving you and therefore willing to make that investment of their time in your business or product to find out what you want them to know. You need your marketing to create the airtime necessary for you to start to forge a relationship.

> if you are a smaller or less well-known business, how do you break through the noise?

Clearly if you're Coca-Cola, Aston Martin, Gucci or Virgin, you're off to a flying start as people already know and have an opinion about you. If you are a smaller or less well-known business, how do you break through the noise?

What you need is social media!

 **brilliant** recap

- Marketing is suffering from falling response rates and it's very difficult to find a formula that works consistently.
- Social media, however, enables you to have intimate conversations with your customers and prospects ... at scale.

PART 1

Why social media works for business

I bet you've heard of Generation X or Generation Y or Generation Z – or the iGeneration – who have been born into a world where they have only ever known email, mobile phones and internet. They are, compared with previous generations, incredibly self-sufficient and, according to the marketing thought leader Brian Solis, almost totally immune to traditional marketing and advertising techniques. They are always connected and, for them, simultaneously using laptop, tablet and phone while watching TV is perfectly natural.

The reason this matters is that these young people are potentially driving behaviours of other generations and are in part why so many of their parents are users of social media. They are desensitising other, older generations to marketing messages and, in order to turn this tide, we need to think about how we position our message in front of these ever-growing segments in a new way. We need a new model, new thinking.

That's where social media comes in: we can get a conversation going at a global level. Talking, listening and answering. Social media is also about relationships. How people interact on the social platforms is just like the way they interact in real life – they chat, they share, they debate, they laugh – and this is in part why social media has got so big so fast, because it exactly mirrors the way we behave offline.

Also because it's about keeping in touch with people – not keeping in touch with demographics, targets or profiles, but *people* – it is an incredibly powerful tool for organisations of all types, helping them to have the conversations that enable relationships, relationships that enable business.

The nature of business is that it's a competitive marketplace. The nature of social media is that it builds trust (rather than being about selling) and this trust is a great basis on which to build rapport and business. An active social media presence means you can better direct your marketing efforts towards the kinds of people you want to engage with, rather than wasting your efforts 'throwing mud at a wall'.

It is worth pointing out, though, that social media isn't a panacea for all ills. It won't, on its own, transform a failing business and it can't compensate for poor quality or changes in fashion, but it can do an awful lot of work for you if you position it in the right way within your business and use it wisely.

Unlike the fundamental shortcoming of traditional marketing techniques, where nobody believes a word you say, with social media you can take the good comments and showcase them to the networks of your clients, which lends them a credibility that traditional marketing could never manage.

CHAPTER 2

The problem with traditional marketing

Traditional marketing has a problem: all of our marketing is created to push *our* message out. We are conditioned into thinking that people arrive at our websites or open our emails wanting to read about us, but this is old thinking.

Most marketing communications campaigns look like the one in Figure 2.1.

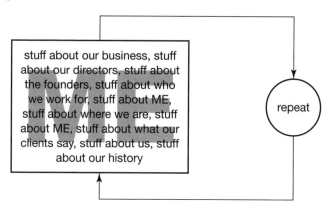

Figure 2.1 Most marketing strategies

Social media marketing is different because, unlike your traditional marketing, which is about broadcasting or sending your message out, social media is two-way, it is a conversation.

social media is two-way, it is a conversation

It enables businesses, for the first time, to talk to their customers in a practical and efficient way, but moreover it enables them to 'talk to' rather than 'shout at'. It is an opportunity to engage clients and prospects in a way never before possible and to forge close relationships with them based on trust, knowledge and understanding – but it has its downside too.

In an always-on culture, getting back to people quickly is vital. If somebody asks a question on a social platform, they expect an answer ... and fast. So putting in place resources and tools to make this possible is very important.

> in an always-on culture, getting back to people quickly is vital

Of course, there are risks, too. Hardly a day goes by without a story about someone having done something stupid on Facebook or Twitter.

Get it right, though, and there's nothing like it. Reduced marketing costs, greater customer insight, a more loyal customer base, better brand recognition, more business, better customer retention, shorter customer purchase cycles, greater staff morale ... the list is long.

CHAPTER 3

Why social media is the marketing of the future

When a contact of mine (Dave Smith) writes a comment about me on either his profile or my profile it is shown to everyone in my network and everyone in his network too (see Figure 3.1). The reason that this is such an important point is that if Dave is in your network, there's a strong possibility you know who he is. If he then starts making positive comments about a supplier, in this case me, there's a much higher chance of you reading those comments and responding to them because you already have a degree of trust in Dave.

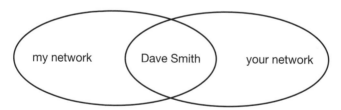

Figure 3.1 Network overlap

Secondly, the compounding effect of your network's network is really quite extraordinary. If you take Facebook, for example, the average number of friends is 130 (on LinkedIn and Twitter this number is typically much higher). So, if you can encourage all of the people in your network (130) to comment (in a nice way) about something you've done or said, it will be showcased to each of their networks (130 friends).

That means you will effectively be receiving a third-party endorsement on your network's network, which is your 130 friends *multiplied* by their 130 friends – so 16,900 people.

> you will effectively be receiving a third-party endorsement on your network's network

That's an exciting prospect for any business.

Something else that you should consider and another big difference between social media and other communications channels is cost scaling. With traditional marketing and communications channels the cost of the audience that you want to access is a direct function of the size of the audience. However, social media is different. The cost of placing your message in front of people doesn't vary with the audience size – if you use your fans on Facebook (once you have built your following), the cost is the same whether you're talking to ten, ten thousand or ten million people.

 **brilliant** tip

Social media *is not free*! That is a fallacy. Yes, there are no media costs (newspaper column inches or radio segments), but there is a cost: time. If you're doing it well you will be spending quite a lot of your time doing it. However, don't fret – later on you'll see just how cost-effective this can be as a marketing and communications channel.

CHAPTER 4

Overarching principles that you must remember

Whether you're new to social media or not, there are some clear principles you must abide by in order to get the most out of it. At this point, let's go back to the very beginning of what social media is there to do.

How it works

In essence, all social media platforms are there to enable sharing of content (ideas, images, news, videos), either with everyone or a pre-approved group of friends or contacts. It's important that you don't forget these people are your 'friends' (whether you've met them or not). Also remember that your online friends do not necessarily have to be people you'd invite to come and stay with you, but they are people you've met (in real life or just online), found (by searching for them or having them pointed out by one of your friends) or just stumbled upon by chance (and in the world of social networking, like in life, 'chance' is a very powerful tool).

> in the world of social networking, like in life, 'chance' is a very powerful tool

Generally the way that most social networks deliver this content is by what could perhaps be described as a chronological cascade.

This 'cascade' is probably the first thing that you see when you log on. It usually takes the form of a series of snippets of what people are doing and what they've said and it is drawn from the individuals you have placed in your contacts or friends list. It's worth noticing that against each of these snippets is a thumbnail image of the person who posted it.

Usually, the content will be delivered in the form of the most recent at the top and the oldest at the bottom. You can keep scrolling back and back and back, often for many months. The main differences between the different networks are these.

- *Are they open or closed?* If the network is 'open', I can follow you without you having to agree to it. YouTube, Twitter and Facebook Business Pages are examples of this. If I cause problems, there is usually some mechanism for blocking me from seeing content any more, but for the most part the networks are created to share content as widely as possible. If a network is 'closed', I send you a connection/friend request and you either accept or refuse. If we are connected, we can freely share between us, but inherently we are sharing only with those people we have added/accepted into our networks – Facebook and LinkedIn are examples of this.

> networks are created to share content as widely as possible

- *What's being shared?* YouTube is videos, Twitter is 140 characters, Pinterest and Flickr are photos, Facebook is a combination of stuff. Some of the sites have quite a strong protocol about what is generally shared and what isn't.

- *The degrees of comment possible.* Some networks, such as Twitter, allow for the redistribution of content and replying to the person who posted the content, but not much else. Facebook, meanwhile, allows people to flag something, as in 'like' it, or to leave a comment against it, in the form of text or image or video.

Make it count

As you scan down the list of updates on your profile, your eye is probably drawn to those posted by some people (and drawn away from those posted by others). This happens because you've been programmed. If you read an update from 'Peter' and it's worthwhile, then you read another from him and it's also good, then another and another, it teaches you through repetition that Peter's updates are worth reading. If, however, they're not very good, it teaches you that too. As time passes you can't help but look out for the updates that experience has shown you are worth reading. Therefore make sure that whatever you post is worth the time and trouble of the person who reads it.

Now, don't get me wrong, it doesn't have to be dull and boring. A good mix is what's required here or something that helps me feel that I've really got to know you.

A great example of this is a friend of mine, June Cory. She runs a company called My Mustard and it is one of the UK's top Google AdWords agencies. She's very active on Twitter, LinkedIn and Facebook and the majority of her posts are jokes and funny comments. As a result of making people smile she has a thriving business and she manages their expectations – she seems like she's great fun and, when you meet her, she is!

Share your best advice

Traditional marketing communications don't work any more, as I've said, and a key reason is credibility. Very few people or organisations are credible. They're all too busy *telling* people why they're good, and we're growing immune to this. Social media provides an opportunity to *show* people why you're good. Take your best

> social media provides an opportunity to *show* people why you're good

advice and tell everybody. I know that this seems a bit counter-intuitive but consider these points and the truth about them.

- *That's my idea, I can't just give it away.* You are not the only business that has had this idea (usually), so the chances are your client/prospect is going to hear it from somewhere … better that it's you because at least you can gain the kudos from telling them.

- *What if readers decide to take my idea and do it themselves?* I would suggest that if they are prepared to have a go at doing it themselves, were they ever really going to pay you to do it? If they appreciate an expert doing things for them, they will be back; if their time is less valuable than money, they would never be comfortable getting you to do the job for them if there was any possibility of doing it in-house.

- *I need to guard that technique in case my competitors use it.* They probably already have the technique. Think about how you behave – if you ever pay for an expert to do something for you, if they're really good the first thing you do when they're gone is share everything you learned with your network because you want to help them. This is what everyone does … including your clients. If you push your best work out into the public domain, it's you who's doing the pushing and it can go out with your branding and contact details on it, flying the flag for your business and showing people exactly how good you are. Showing them … not telling them.

Don't sell!

These people are your friends. You should be trying to win their trust and deepen your relationship with them. If you sell to them you are betraying the trust that you have worked so hard to build.

 **tip**

So, there are a few rules – these are not general points of protocol, these are fundamental truths of social media that are proven time and time again.

Don't sell.

Don't babble.

Don't talk drivel.

Use your brain.

Think before pressing 'send'.

Numbers aren't everything

Social media is *really* big. Facebook has 1 billion members. Ask yourself, 'Do I want a billion new customers tomorrow?' The answer is probably 'no'. You don't want a billion, a million, a thousand and, depending on what your business is, you probably don't even want a hundred new customers. Most businesses, certainly smaller ones, couldn't even handle a hundred telephone enquiries. So if this is the case it's great news because it means you can be

> you can be incredibly selective about who you want to work with

incredibly selective about who you want to work with. You can be very honest about who you are and what your strengths and weaknesses are because you're not trying to be all things to all people ... you only want to work with the people who *really* want to work with you.

The key learning here is honesty. If you don't claim to do everything or to be a full-service business, that's probably OK. Just focus on the stuff that you're really good at and the stuff you really like ... and then tell people about it. Let them see your passion for these key services and let them get swept along with your enthusiasm.

CHAPTER 5

Getting started

S o, a successful social media presence, if you boil it down to its very essence, is made up of four parts:

- strategy
- passive social presence
- active social participation
- monitoring and refining.

You could almost treat this like a mini marketing strategy for your business; so let's have a look at each of those parts in turn.

Strategy

Clearly, like with any other area of business, it is crucial to have a plan. Without a clear social media strategy it is unlikely that you will have considered how to control what people say, what happens if it all goes wrong or how to measure the success that you're having. You need to recognise that you can't be on every social media platform all of the time and, while social media platforms are the place to be, well, social, you must have an objective in mind. You must be clear about what you're hoping to achieve. You must decide what you're going to do … then do it. Failure to do this may well leave you having invested a huge amount of time in conversations and relationships, but without having any benefit from having done it.

brilliant tip

Plan a strategy. It doesn't have to be detailed or complex to start with, but just dabbling is unlikely to deliver the benefits that you hope for. A simple plan that says what you're going to do, on how many networks, and how much time you're going to invest might be enough to begin with.

Steps in creating a strategy would be:

- choosing platforms
- setting guidelines
- use of language and tone of voice
- setting goals and long-term objectives
- training
- measuring success
- allocating resources and budgets
- monitoring comments
- maximising amplification

- responsibilities
- creating and/or sourcing content.

These are not all of the points that you may want to cover in your social media strategy, and not all businesses are going to want to cover all of these points, but it's as good a place as any to start.

The key is to develop a strategy that works for your business. It may be just a couple of pages or it may be a significant document – either way it's *your* strategy and that's the most important thing.

In social media, more than in any other communications discipline, you must try to innovate and, if you see another individual or company having success in the social media world, try to identify why they're successful ... then do something else! There's no prize for coming second and you certainly don't want to be 'the company that are a bit like Company X', so you need to find your own voice and do something fresh.

Choosing platforms

The first and initially the biggest decision that you're going to need to make has to be: 'On which platforms should I focus my effort?' See Part 2 for all the information you'll need.

Setting guidelines

Within smaller businesses, often everybody understands what the business is trying to achieve with social media. The nature of small businesses is that often people need to wear many hats and, in my experience of such businesses, everyone takes responsibility for marketing the business. However, in larger businesses people usually have a much less general role – they specialise in certain areas and

> the larger the company, the more important some social media guidelines are

disciplines and they sometimes do not possess that overall view of what needs to be done and what their responsibilities are to achieve this. So the larger the company, the more important some social media guidelines are.

The job of guidelines is to set boundaries for everyone to work within. Generally they should be as short as possible (half a page rather than six pages) and should encourage people to be active and chatty on the networks while upholding whatever your company brand values are. It's worth remembering that in asking your staff to use their own social networks to talk about and promote the business, you are in fact asking them a favour, so don't be too prescriptive.

If you have a specific marketing function that will be administering the company Facebook page and Twitter account, clearly you can be both more prescriptive and, more importantly, more results-focused. Try to empower the staff and encourage them to focus on keeping conversations going for as long as possible with a speedy response rather than just growing the number of followers.

In each case, though, it's important that the overall sense of purpose is retained.

Use of language and tone of voice

If you are a micro business, probably many of the relationships are created and owned by key members of the team and that is what's often being sold. So maintaining a sense of who you are as an individual is really important. Be honest, be forthright (perhaps temper your more militant views from time to time), but generally be yourself.

Clearly, though, this advice can't always work for large businesses. Sometimes there needs to be some control of language to keep the dialogue 'on brand'. Coutts Bank, the old established bank that's favoured by the super-rich and the royal family, has a completely different tone of voice from Virgin Money, for example, and the various branding agencies work very hard to create this feeling by carefully picking the right words and phrases to support the overall branding strategy.

This can cause problems for larger businesses because social media is generally a spontaneous conversation, so if this is tempered by having to check every phrase against a brand dictionary or seek approval from the brand guardian, much of the naturalness created on the networks can be lost.

This is a challenge that each business will need to come to terms with in its own way.

It's worth remembering that most people aren't stupid (although they sometimes make stupid mistakes). As a business you're happy to let your staff talk to your customers, either face to face or by phone, and having those same staff chat on social media channels is really no different.

Setting goals

One of the most crucial parts of every plan (social media, marketing, business) is setting goals. Identifying what is a reasonable thing to try to achieve and then examining why the business is or is not on track to achieve this is one of the fundamental tools to use to drive the business forward.

Long-term objectives

Social media success probably isn't going to come overnight. Sometimes it does – I have worked with clients who have won fantastic new contracts through social channels literally within a few hours of starting, but this is the exception rather than the rule. It's very nice when it happens, but it doesn't happen all that often and you certainly can't rely on it happening for you.

So you need to consider what you want your social media presence to look like in 3 months, 12 months, 24 months ... and plan to achieve it.

You might say that in 24 months you want your social media activity to drive an additional 1,000 new visitors to your website, it should also have established you as the major player in your industry and the barometer for this will be that you are speaking at one conference each month.

> you *must* plan in order to succeed in social media

You need to decide what the future of your business looks like and then break down that goal into simple, easy-to-take steps. You *must* plan in order to succeed in social media. If you don't, you can absolutely rely on the fact that your competitors will.

Training

You can't expect people to intuitively know what to do. It doesn't matter if you've employed people who have a huge number of Facebook friends or are 'always on Twitter' – you need to tell them what's expected of them. They need to know how to monitor what's happening in the social space to both your brand and your competitors. They need to understand

> monitor what's happening in the social space to both your brand and your competitors

how to identify key influencers and amplifiers for your industry and those who share interesting and valuable content that you in turn can re-share.

Most importantly they need to understand how to monitor the results of their efforts.

It's no use whatsoever being busy and sending lots of tweets and updates if you don't know whether or not anyone is reading what you're saying. Being able to see the effect that your social efforts are generating in terms of network traffic, conversations and web traffic is crucial, because without this you can't refine what you're doing or even know if you're barking up the wrong tree altogether.

The only way your staff will know how to do this is if they are either trained or spend a long time learning it for themselves. So make sure you have in place a plan of how to train them to do things well and also how to keep abreast of changes that will impact what they do.

Measuring success

Measuring the fruits of your labours is vital. I often say to clients, 'Do you think that there will be a difference in success rates of a.m./p.m. updates or of questions/statements?' Of course, the answer is 'yes'. If you're not measuring the results of what you do, though, how can you possibly hope to know which of the two works the best for your audience? Clearly you shouldn't be doing something one way if there's a better way to do it and the only way you know how to do it is to measure both and see the difference.

The great thing about the social space is that because it's digital you can get all the answers in real time. Setting up a management platform such as Sprout Social or HootSuite will enable you easily to know for certain what people are engaging with and change what you do to maximise the results you get.

Allocating resources

Somebody has to do it. It won't happen by chance or because you want it to. Some of my larger clients have found that their activity has been quite hit and miss because they have not allocated appropriate resources internally to run their social presence on an ongoing basis.

Someone has to take ownership of the social presence. Someone has to manage it and someone has to be responsible for making sure that what is going on at ground level – the individual interactions – is driving benefit for the business' big picture. This won't happen by accident and if someone isn't answerable for social activity it simply won't happen because there will be something more pressing that needs to be done *now*.

A single tweet or update isn't going to make a massive difference to the business in itself, whereas a problem with a client might. With social media every tweet matters, though, in terms of the benefit that will be derived from the compounding effect of regular little things. Just think, if you go to the gym today, will you be fitter tomorrow? Not so you'd notice. If you go for a week, will you be healthier? Probably not. How about if you go to the gym every day for two years? Oh yes!

Every little action adds to the effect of every other and it is this 'compounding benefit' that makes the difference, particularly in social media.

Allocating budgets

Social media is free, isn't it? In short, no. There's your time and there may even be a cash cost, perhaps developing a Facebook app, some design agency time to create backgrounds or graphics or perhaps some studio time with a photographer for your profile photos. All of this needs to be considered.

Of course, the biggest cost with social media is in execution – the people cost of interacting with comments, writing tweets and sourcing content. This cost must be budgeted, because if it isn't there's a very real risk that the social media action your business needs won't ever get done because the people who should be answering comments and engaging in the real-time conversations with customers and prospects will in fact be too busy doing other things.

Monitoring comments

When people leave comments or respond to your updates it's really important to deal with this speedily. If they've asked a question, you need to answer. If something positive has been said, thank them for it. If they've made a complaint or a criticism, you need to jump on it and deal with the problem quickly to try and turn something negative into something positive.

Maximising amplification

Everybody who connects with you could be a prospective customer. Everybody who leaves comments needs to have them answered – not just for the sake of that customer but for all your customers who need to see that you're being reactive, human and friendly with those approaching you. However, clearly some people are, in the social space at least, worth investing a little bit more time in.

> everybody who connects with you could be a prospective customer

Every time that you have a comment to field or a question to answer, before you crack on and write whatever your response is going to be, try to have a look at the person who has made the comment. Have they got a particularly large or engaged network? Do they seem to be particularly influential?

As you will have read earlier in the book, one of the great benefits of social media is social leverage – using the people in your network to promote you to their networks. Clearly a person who has a particularly large or highly engaged network is significantly more attractive than a person with a small network. So, all things being equal, choose the person with the larger network if you need to make a choice about which one gets the best reply.

For example, if Susan has a network of 100 people and makes a comment on your profile, it will be shown (but not necessarily seen) by her 100 connections. If Jane has a network of 2,000 people, there is the opportunity for anything she posts on your profile to be seen by 20 times as many people.

Picking the people who give you maximum amplification of your message will help establish the largest social leverage you can get. Failing to answer these people in a timely and appropriate manner could have severe consequences.

Responsibilities

As with any other business function that has variables (in this case the public), it's really important to have in place a process to deal with any 'issues' that may occur. There needs to be a clear chain of command to deal with genuine complaints, and quickly. Having a manager who is able to take a dispassionate view of a situation and who has some training in customer service will be necessary to turn any negative situation into a positive.

Of course, it isn't just risks. It's important that if an obvious sales opportunity presents itself, the person handling the conversation can alert someone from the sales department swiftly so that the chances of closing the deal are as high as possible.

Creating content

Social media, as I will say many times during the course of the book, is a content-hungry animal. It needs constant feeding and while you don't need to originate all of the content that you share across your social networks, you certainly need to originate some of it. Tasking part of the business to produce regular blog posts or any other kind of content may prove to be far more difficult than you imagine at the moment.

You may well find that you have a queue of people initially who want to try their hand at writing content, but this (in my experience) won't last. So there needs to be buy-in and commitment from the people who are going to keep providing content – and it needs to be good.

Sourcing content

Thankfully, your social channels won't be just for your own content. You can gain a huge amount of kudos and benefit from sourcing and sharing great content that others have produced (be careful not to steal it and pretend it's yours, of course). This is particularly handy as it's a lot easier to find good content than it is to write it, but you need to know where to look.

On each of your social networks where you have chosen to follow or connect with people, they will probably be sharing their good content (and, of course, content that they've found) and this is a ready source of things that you yourself can share … but you have to read it first.

Social media is not a broadcast channel. You are not there simply to talk, hoping that others will listen. You should be listening too, and if you find some good content from these people, share it – acknowledge them and thank them, because a) it's nice to do so and b) this will come back to you as a huge benefit down the line as you will see in Part 3 – 'Making social media work harder'.

Passive social presence

As you start to get into using social media you will probably notice that what you do in the social media space is divided into two distinct areas – passive and active.

Failing to complete your profile (with every bit of information you can) is rather like going to a networking meeting and handing out blank rectangles of paper as your 'business cards' – it just doesn't make sense.

Passive social presence

This is the footprint that you leave on your social media profiles, the bit that others use to find you and connect to you ... or not. This is a vital part of what you need to do to achieve success in the social media world. This is the (mostly) static page that is your description of who you are or what you do. It may (depending on which social media platform) contain links to your website, a photo of you, a company logo, video clips, descriptions and much more. Getting this right is the first step to social media success.

On every single social media platform your profile page gives you an opportunity to talk about who you are and what you do – make sure that you take it. This profile page will enable people to identify whether you are the person they're looking for or you offer the service that they need.

> your profile page gives you an opportunity to talk about who you are and what you do

On all of the social networks there are huge numbers of people with the same name or service as you and you need to make it as easy as possible for people to see whether you are (or are not) the person they're looking for, so clarity in everything is paramount – clear photo, clear description, clear business offering, everything.

Placing a picture on the profile is a prerequisite of being found by people who have met you. I am *not* the only Adam Gray in the world, so it's really important that when someone looks for me they can see that it is *me* and not Adam Gray the hairdresser or Adam Gray the award-winning chef or even Adam Gray the up-and-coming Rodeo star, but *me*.

You must make sure that what you write is as full, complete and compelling as you can possibly make it. Too often these areas are left blank, which is potentially confusing to the visitor, a missed opportunity for you and a lost chance to leverage the search engine optimisation (SEO) benefits that social media brings. When you write the information you place on your profile it needs to clearly articulate who you are, what you do, why you're passionate about it and why I should engage with you about it.

brilliant definition

Search engine optimisation (SEO)

This is the science of creating web pages and content in such a way that search engines place it near to the top of the search results they deliver. For example, my goal is to ensure that 'Adam Gray' appears on the first page (or as near as possible) of results for terms such as 'Social Media Expert UK'.

This SEO benefit should not be underestimated. Companies that have successful digital marketing strategies often spend significant amounts of time and money ensuring they rank well in search results. Traditionally this has been delivered through a series of special pages attached to their websites created to 'catch Google's eye'. However, for some time Google has also been using other methods to rank pages and one of these methods is (yes, you guessed it) social media. The reason I talk about Google specifically rather than 'search engines' is because it is the biggest (by far), with over twice the number of searches every day/week/month as all the other search engines combined. While your company may be first in the rankings of ASK or AOL or even Yahoo!, this is likely to be of less benefit than being first on Google.

There are a few little tricks that we'll cover in the individual platform sections, but for now you need to park your bashful modest self and start to think about what you're going to write about yourself that makes you sound like an expert and someone who really cares ... and then write it, with pride.

Active social participation

Once you have your profiles complete and they reflect well on you and your business, you need to start to make use of them. There is a chance that people will find you and connect anyway, but why take a chance? Go out and get the people you want – turn this passive social presence into active social participation.

You need to begin to make yourself visible. You need to start to connect with people and begin to have conversations with them.

It's really easy, but you need to remember a few commonsense rules. Imagine being part of an online social network as like being at a party. Be courteous, be charming, don't always be talking about yourself, show interest ... it's simple really.

At this 'social media party' you need to be up and talking to people rather than sitting in a corner looking sorry for yourself. Connect to people, then start to engage them in conversation. But how?

In pretty much all social networks the person you're connecting with will be aware of the fact that you've connected with them. On LinkedIn/Facebook you will have asked them to connect, on Twitter/Facebook pages you can just follow (or 'like') them and they will get a notification. Either way they will know.

Once you are in their network you will potentially be seen by them, but 'potentially' isn't good enough. If they have 100, 1,000, possibly 10,000 in their network, the chances of being seen are at best slim. If everyone (including you) posts an update once every day, you will need to be very special to be noticed, but it can be done.

you will need to be very special to be noticed, but it can be done

At this point you might well be saying, 'This sounds like an awful lot of work', and indeed it is, but it is a huge opportunity. Consider the enormous utilisation of your resources with:

Business networking

Most businesses need to have conversations with their customers and prospects. This isn't always the case, but usually it is. These days many businesses choose to have these conversations face to face through networking, events and conferences and without a doubt this is the most effective way of converting people into advocates and winning business. However, it's very costly. Conversations usually mean that one of your staff is going to have to be in a room with one of my staff, so every hour of meeting costs both you and me an hour's worth of pay ... or worse still, an hour when we haven't been billing our clients.

If a business charges £75/hour for its time and the cost for staffing and overheads is, say, £30/hour – typically, the annual costs for membership of a business networking breakfast group may look like this:

membership of the group: £500/pa

breakfast costs: £10/week

attendance: every week

length of meeting: 2 hours

travel: 30 minutes each way

So:

3 hours/week × 50 weeks × £75/hour = £11,250 in opportunity costs (missed billings) + £1,000 in cash

Based on making £45/hour profit that means each year you need to bill 272 hours at full rate to break even! (That's more than five hours every week.) When you consider even the better networkers probably only talk to three or four people each week in a meaningful way, that means it's necessary to convert in excess of 100 per cent of your conversations to run at a profit.

Now, I'm not saying that networking events aren't worthwhile, because they definitely are, but there needs to be a way of making sure that you have coffee only with people who are amenable to your message. Everyone who builds and retains relationships as part of their customer acquisition process needs to drink a lot of coffee.

Many of these coffee meetings aren't sales meetings, they're relationship-building meetings. They're about making sure that people don't forget who you are, so when they find a prospect for you or are ready themselves to purchase, they don't go elsewhere. However, much of this can be done remotely. Much of this can be done more frequently, more personally and more effectively by *not* having coffee but by having an online conversation. Remember that as you're bonding with this person online, their friends can see what sort of person you are … further spreading your influence and contact base.

PART 2

Choosing and using platforms

With so many different potential platforms for you to use you're going to need to think about where you want to focus your effort. You can't be everywhere, so before you take the plunge and start signing up for different platforms, consider which are most appropriate for you and your business.

As I said earlier, you must fill out all the available fields on each and every social platform that you join. Remember that failing to complete your profile will not only diminish how effective the network will be for you but, it might also actually be damaging because any prospective client who sees your profile incomplete will start to make assumptions – and life tells us that the assumptions people jump to are rarely the ones we want them to.

With this in mind, you are probably going to want to collect together a few bits to make the sign-up process more straightforward – things such as company logo, a short description of what the business does, photographs and maps will all be needed, so why not get them together before you begin? Remember that merely signing up for the various networks but failing to fill out the information is like handing people blank squares of paper and calling them business cards – you must put down every piece of information that you can.

CHAPTER 6

Selecting the right social media platforms

One of the biggest initial decisions that you're going to need to make is, 'Which social media platforms should I be using?' This is a very important choice and it isn't one to be taken lightly.

Because each of the platforms is going to require some understanding of the pros and cons, setting up and ongoing management, it's certainly worth trying to understand why you should be on each platform. If you can't really see how one of these platforms would work for your business for the moment, then I would probably suggest that you focus your efforts elsewhere for the time being. Even the biggest names in the world of social media aren't on all of the platforms – they have made choices about which platforms suit their business, their audience and their workflow, and these are decisions that you are possibly going to have to make too.

> even the biggest names in the world of social media aren't on all of the platforms

Of course, there are some obvious choices for the shortlist of social media platforms to join – Facebook, LinkedIn, Twitter, Google+, YouTube, Flickr, Pinterest and perhaps others that have caught your attention.

⟋ ⟩brilliant impact

When deciding which of the available platforms you should use you might want to give some thought to the following.

Are there any industry-specific platforms?

How many members does it have (bigger is often better)?

Does it have the functionality you need?

Are there any costs involved?

Which networks are your clients and prospects using?

Does your business produce content from some of these by default?

One thing you can be certain of, though, is that you will not be able to be on all of them in a meaningful way ... certainly not at the beginning.

The best resource that I have seen for you to appreciate just how wide a choice you have is the Conversation Prism, shown in Figure 6.1. You can view this at **www.theconversation-prism.com** (thanks to Brian Solis for the use of this). I'm not advocating joining all of these, but this is a great place to see what the choices are.

Once you have made the decision about which platforms to start on, it's time to set up your profiles and start using them. However, remember, it's better to be skilled and active on one network than inactive and naive on many!

A key point here, and one I will keep mentioning throughout the book, is that social media (across all platforms) is about being social. It's a place for people to come together and share ideas and engage with each other, and the value that you can get from using the various platforms is based on what you *give*, not what you take.

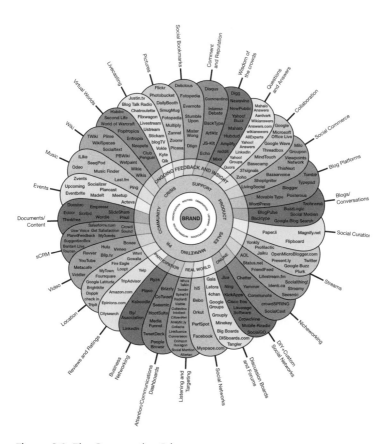

Figure 6.1 The Conversation Prism   *Source:* Brian Solis and JESS3

The rest of this section in the book examines each of the major social media platforms, outlines what they can do (and what they can't do), how to set up and begin using them and some of the tricks I have learned over the years that with hindsight seem very obvious but not at the time when I was grappling with the problem of why things weren't working as I perhaps hoped they would.

I'm sure I've already said this, but I'll say it again anyway. There are elements that I will repeat again and again in this book – the main mistakes, albeit obvious, people tend to make.

In reality the use of social media is natural and surprisingly simple, but we overly complicate it by applying marketing principles and sales theories to it ... and they just don't work.

the use of social media is natural and surprisingly simple

So if you think that you've heard me say something before ... you probably have!

Now let's have a look at each of the major platforms in turn and examine what they're for, what this means to you and your business and how you can start to use them effectively.

brilliant tip

Pick a small number of social media platforms to use initially while you get comfortable rather than setting up a dozen different accounts badly and using none of them.

CHAPTER 7

LinkedIn

What is it?

LinkedIn is the largest business network on the internet. As I write this, LinkedIn has just passed the 200 million members mark and is signing up more than 2 new members every second. LinkedIn is growing exponentially – to sign up the first 1 million members took 18 months and to sign up the next 1 million took just nine days!

How does it work?

If you've ever been to a networking group you'll probably have a pretty good idea of how LinkedIn works. LinkedIn members are part of a virtual networking forum to meet and connect with other individuals and, with luck, forge relationships with them that will ultimately lead to business.

In many ways it's a lot easier than going to real-life networking groups as you don't need to walk up to people and introduce yourself, you don't need to deliver your one-minute elevator pitch to the group and you never need to give a detailed presentation about what your business does.

This means that people who are not comfortable speaking in front of an audience can still have conversations and meet new contacts but without the stress of public speaking.

However, the consequence of this is that, because there isn't this distillation of what your business does, or indeed the imperative for you to deliver it, sometimes people fail to understand what you do or whether or not you are good at it.

What are the benefits?

LinkedIn gives its members the chance to connect with an almost limitless number of people and, once someone has accepted your connection request, there is a conduit open for an ongoing conversation between the two of you – every time one of you updates your status or makes any account changes, it appears in the other's newsfeed.

You can also message one another (avoiding email and all of the spam that it so often gets masked by) and you can recommend, introduce and share information.

There are also huge numbers of industry- and subject-specific groups that you can join and interact within ... or perhaps just watch, listen and learn.

Whatever your need from social media, LinkedIn is rapidly becoming the place where everyone needs to be. The point has already been reached where not being on LinkedIn says a lot about you.

This will probably be the easiest place for novices to begin to forge relationships that have a clear benefit and it's not uncommon to win some business relatively quickly. There is a huge number of business- and marketing-biased features that make the process of meeting, getting to know and converting business relatively straightforward. However, increasingly it is difficult to maintain visibility with large numbers because

> it is difficult to maintain visibility with large numbers because the newsfeed can get clogged up

the newsfeed can get clogged up with huge numbers of status updates and general network activity, which can be quite bland and uninspiring. Do I really care that Clare Smith is now connected to Paul Jones? Probably not.

LinkedIn was the first social network that I joined (although at the time I wasn't quite sure why!) and back then I distinctly remember spending quite a while searching for people I knew who I could connect with and there weren't many. Now, with the membership having increased many thousand-fold, pretty much everyone I need to be connected to is already there. LinkedIn is one of the key platforms for most businesses as it is focused and (politically) acceptable for staff to be on it.

It is free to join, free to use and offers a host of possibilities to connect to professionals who may be able to help you, plus it is a reasonably safe environment – there's little risk and you can pick and choose who you connect to.

So how do I sign up?

LinkedIn is composed of a series of discrete but important elements:

1 Personal profile
2 Company profile/page
3 Links
4 Groups
5 Newsfeed
6 Apps
7 Contacts
8 Jobs
9 Inbox.

brilliant tip

There's no need to be intimidated by LinkedIn, but if you don't do anything else, here is a simple series of steps to get started.

1 Sign up.
2 Upload a photo and fill out all the fields that you can for your profile.
3 Make sure that you include past employment details.
4 Connect to all your colleagues, both past and present.
5 Get into the habit of connecting to every new person you meet.

1 Personal profile

This would best be considered as your CV online. In it you can detail what you do and what you've done and you can gain endorsements and testimonials from people you know. This is an opportunity for you to stand out from the crowd.

A crucial point, and one of the biggest benefits of your LinkedIn profile, is that it is indexed by Google rather than just by the LinkedIn search engine, so what you say on this page will potentially be of huge benefit to your visibility and credibility not just on LinkedIn but on the internet as a whole. When considering what your profile page should say, you need to think about the fact that you have two distinct audiences to appeal to.

The first is the visitor to your page. For the visitor you need to write something that is compelling and flowing. It needs to be written in good English (or whichever language you speak), it needs to tell a good story that makes sense and it needs to demonstrate the service (or product) you're selling is really important to both you and the reader.

This latter point is perhaps the most important. Successful LinkedIn profiles show empathy with the reader's needs and concerns. Saying, 'I'm passionate about bought ledger as this is, in my opinion, the most vital of business functions because ...' is infinitely more appealing to the reader than, 'I'm a bought ledger clerk and I enter figures into the bought ledger'. The latter is factually correct but isn't going to set the world alight.

With your LinkedIn profile you have a short amount of time to make an impression on people – don't squander this window of opportunity. If you're not passionate about what you do, there's no way that the person reading will be either and, with literally thousands of people offering ostensibly the same service literally only a click away, you aren't going to win the business.

> you have a short amount of time to make an impression on people

It's worth saying once again that it needs to tell a good, coherent story. Many people have a career that has meandered a little bit. Perhaps they have had several changes because of industry pressure; perhaps because they've been hunting for what they really want to do. Either way, this needs to be handled with a certain amount of sensitivity.

You need to find a way to tie these things together, such that the transition from one to another is a clear and obvious progression that has been part of a larger overall plan. Pulling this off may not be easy, but you must make an effort as people jump to all sorts of conclusions and it's up to you to make sure that they jump to the conclusions you want!

brilliant tip

If your profile says that you trained as a doctor, you then became a financial adviser, you then changed again to become a gardener, this may well appear to the casual onlooker that you don't have any staying power or commitment and it's only a matter of time before you change and try something else. This needs to be handled with care.

The second audience that you need to appeal to is Google (or any other search engine for that matter). Search engines have one purpose – to deliver to the person who is searching the most relevant results on the internet (or in the case of searching within LinkedIn, on LinkedIn). One of the key ways they do this is by analysing the content of the page.

If you want to be found for being a 'fantastic accountant' it is vital that you have the phrase 'fantastic accountant' on your page. The more times it's there, the more likely you are to be favourably positioned in the search rankings when someone searches for 'fantastic accountant' (assuming the text makes grammatical sense and that it isn't too pushy). Clearly there are a number of points that need to be considered here and the skill in writing a good profile is in balancing these (sometimes) conflicting requirements to make a profile that is both found and acted on.

- Make sure that the people who read your profile page are wowed by your commitment, skill, credibility and perhaps humour to such an extent they want either to connect with you or to pick up the telephone to speak to you.
- Make sure that they get there in the first place! Make the profile as attractive to Google (and others) as you possibly can so that you can start to generate some footfall there. Clearly the best profile in the world is of no use if nobody can find it.
- Make sure that the phrases you want to be found for are phrases your customers are actually looking for and, remember, there's a huge difference in Google's eyes between 'fantastic accountant' and 'fantastic accountants' (keyword analysis - a detailed description can be found at **www.GrayUK.com/brilliant)**.

The personal profile itself has a number of areas that you should fill out. Going through these in turn should help you cover most things and forms a great template to ensure that you don't miss anything.

As a general comment on what you write on the LinkedIn profile (though true of every single network) and what you write in status updates, it should be in a simple, straightforward style and avoid the following.

- Using the third person – the profile is written by you. It is a personal profile, therefore writing it in the third person, e.g. 'Adam Gray has been working in social media', does not make you sound more professional. In fact, you run a very real risk of sounding pompous! If you are not happy saying the exact words to someone, don't write them. It's much better to write, 'I work in social media' – it is more natural, more personal and more engaging.

- Using jargon – avoid using any abbreviations or acronyms. You'd be amazed how few people actually know what they mean – even the ones you think are obvious might not be. This is especially true of people who are going to be buying your products or service. Remember KISS (Keep It Simple Stupid!) – see what I mean?

- Using complex language – don't use 'assist' where 'help' will do, don't use 'pneumonoultramicroscopicsilicovolcano-coniosis' where 'a lung disease' will do. The simpler the word, the less ambiguous it is when used in conversation and, most importantly, the more powerful it is – because we learned simple words at a younger age and therefore they have had more time to develop an emotional meaning for us.

- Being irrelevant – you are hoping that visitors are going to read your profile, so keep it focused. You may be interested to know about my extensive collection of LCD mobile telephone screens ... but I doubt it. Remember why you're writing your information and what conclusion you wish me to draw after having read it.

- Being inappropriate – how do you wish to be perceived through both your profile and your status updates? *Never* swear. I swear quite a lot, but never in front of an audience or in writing. It just doesn't translate well into the business world. Also, how you phrase things needs to reflect how you want your brand to be perceived. 'We are delighted that you've decided to explore our website' is perhaps more appropriate for a 200–year-old bank than a funky surf brand, where 'Alright, good to see you' might be more in keeping with the audience and its expectations.

Summary

This is the bit where you can write in flowing prose about how much you love your job and the clients you work with. This should *not* be a shopping list of skills but some lovely writing from the heart about who you are and why you do what you do. You should not talk about your job (per se) in this area but about your career and, most importantly, about you. This is the area where you should really let fly with your emotions! Many people struggle with this as they feel embarrassed to talk about themselves in a positive light (as they think it sounds arrogant), but, remember, this will be the first thing visitors see and it is vital that you stop them in their tracks and encourage them to read on.

Skills and expertise

In this section you need to detail what your 'superpowers' are. If you are a management accountant then add this skill. Once you have done this, a click on the flag that has appeared will allow you to add a level of proficiency and the number of years of experience. A word of caution here: you can't be an expert at everything and experts are not made overnight. Be realistic. If you are believable about your skills then people will tend to believe other things you say.

> you can't be an expert at everything and experts are not made overnight

Visitors to your profile can now confirm if they have experience of your skill in a particular area and give an endorsement of this. This is rather like a scoreboard. So, '25 people have endorsed David as an accountant' clearly demonstrates there are 25 people prepared to confirm that David is indeed a good accountant. However, it's not unreasonable to assume that these are people who are passing acquaintances rather than close business contacts as they have chosen to tick a box rather than to write a full-blown recommendation for you.

Experience

Here you should detail every major role that you've had. This is really important because many of your best connections in your network may well be ones you know as either colleagues or clients from previous roles. Reforging and strengthening these relationships may well pay dividends ... perhaps sooner than you think. As an example: I have given some help to a large law firm based in Ipswich. One of its partners in the employment law team had been a LinkedIn user for some time, but decided to ramp up the firm's connections and looked back through its employment history, connecting with an ex-boss. Immediately on connection the ex-boss said, 'It's funny you should connect now, I've just identified a serious HR issue that you may be able to help with' and, with that, commissioned £10,000 of work that very day. Of course, it would be unreasonable to assume that things always happen like this, but they do from time to time and more often than you may think.

When you're filling out this section you probably need to develop a system to ensure you cover the stuff you want to say in a way that works for all your past roles. On my LinkedIn profile, for example, I've settled on a brief description of what the business does, what I do (or did) within the business, clients I have worked with and what my specialities are. This means that I can have a certain repetition of content from one role to the next, helping me to tie them together in a meaningful way for anyone who wants to read back over my history.

brilliant tip

Overall on your profile, one of the most important things to achieve is 100 per cent profile completeness. This will make sure that a) LinkedIn gives you the best possible visibility and b) visitors who arrive there can find all the information to make the appropriate decision about you.

Projects

Here you can add projects that you're involved in and those within your network who are also working on the same projects. Your connections on LinkedIn can see who you're collaborating with on those projects. For the moment, that's about it.

Education

This is self-explanatory. At first glance there may not be a huge benefit in entering your education details, particularly if you left university 25 years ago. However, it's all too easy to lose touch with people and it may well be that some of the people you went to school with are now in positions of power within some great companies. Connecting with them on LinkedIn and beginning a dialogue can only be a good thing, and leveraging that relationship will invariably prove to be a lot easier than starting a relationship with someone new.

Recommendations

An interesting element of human nature is that we're all inherently quite bashful (well, most of us are) and when it comes to writing about our expertise we generally wouldn't be particularly verbose or gushing about how good we are. Thankfully we don't feel that way about others! On LinkedIn the recommendations you're likely to get from others are far more flattering than anything you would ever write about yourself. One of the things that you will have to overcome, though, is bashfulness about asking others to recommend you. It's OK ... honestly! If a supplier or colleague had done some work for you and you were happy with it, how would you feel if they asked you for a testimonial? Most people would be happy to recommend someone if the person in question had done a good job. Your clients will be happy to recommend you too.

Additional information

This section includes groups, interests, websites, etc. Here you can bring in the outbound links from your profile along with any more personal information you may choose to share.

From a technical perspective the outbound links are a huge benefit. They are indexed by Google and therefore pointing them at your website means that Google registers them as inbound links ... the more of these you have, the better. It's probably worth mentioning that setting up these links for maximum benefit will be achieved not by using the generic 'my website' option but instead selecting the 'other' option from the dropdown menu, then adding 'fantastic accountant' or whatever seems most appropriate. Better still, don't point this at your homepage but point it at your 'fantastic accountant' page.

> an important part of developing relationships is building 'rapport' with the other party

As far as personal information goes, clearly this isn't important, right? Wrong! It's no secret that a vital part of developing relationships is building 'rapport' with the other party. If you are a keen golfer it will immediately give you some common ground on which to begin building a relationship if the other person is also a keen golfer – as a word of warning, choose things that others are unlikely to find offensive and where possible are not too niche.

The 'groups' listing shows which groups you are a member of. As in so many areas of human behaviour, being part of the right group(s) may help add just the smallest amount of credibility – not enough in itself to win a piece of business, but, with your LinkedIn profile, as with so much in business, success is often measured by the sum of a series of tiny, incremental improvements.

Contact details

Your business email and telephone number here would be a good idea. I know that sounds obvious, but you'd be amazed at the number of clients who somehow think that their contact details should be private. Clearly, your contact details should be obvious to everyone ... if you want people to give you business, that is!

Although your personal profile is your CV online, it doesn't mean that you're looking for a job. It's an opportunity for you to articulate why you are credible and trustworthy. Remember, people buy from people, so you are the best sales tool your company has

2 Company profile/page

Rather like the personal profile, the company page is a chance to talk in a positive way about the company. It also acts as a central point for all the company's employees so as a visitor to the profile I can see who works there and what their roles are.

As a business there are several different areas of the company profile.

- *Home.* This is the area for you to write about the company; it also shows visitors any recent updates that have been posted by the company. Visitors can subscribe to these updates by 'following' the company so they can keep abreast of what it does.

- *Careers.* This is where you can post any job vacancies that the business might have. It also lists all staff members who are on LinkedIn.

- *Products.* If the business offers specific products and services, you would list those here. It could be consultancy or a book or any other defined offering. Visitors and customers can then comment on and recommend these if appropriate.

- *Insights.* This is where personnel changes (new hires, departures and promotions), similar companies and other network information would be displayed.

One of the most important, but often overlooked, things that you should do with this section is leverage keyword recognition (word analysis - a detailed description can be found at **www.GrayUK.com/brilliant**). Once you have chosen the keywords that you want to be found for, you need to write a short, compelling, keyword-rich description of what the business does and why it's so special. This should then be copied into the lower half of every employee's 'summary' section on their personal profile. This will ensure that a) there is uniformity among staff as to what the company does and b) the maximum visibility will be gained on Google.

The nature of a company rather than a personal page is that it's likely to get far less traffic and far fewer subscribers. However, it is another touch point for customers to discover you.

3 Links

Each employee has a maximum of three possible links from their profile. The company has just one. It therefore makes sense for the company page link to point at your website's homepage. For each of the individuals on LinkedIn it's possible to be significantly more targeted. I, for example, have three main strands to my business: social media consultancy, social media training and social media speaking. My website has a page for each of these three services. So I have used the three possible links, one to each of those pages – 'social media consultant', 'social media speaker' and 'social media training'. The links are worded this way by design. I know it would be grammatically better to put 'social media trainer' but there are 23 times as many searches for 'social media training' as there are for 'social media trainer'. It would be worth you checking what the popular search phrases are in your case and optimising not just your LinkedIn profile but all of your social profiles and your website too by using the Google Keyword tool.

Finally, with regard to links, it is worth noticing that you have a unique URL on LinkedIn – by default this will be your name followed by a random string of numbers and letters. There is an option to change this – pick something personal, catchy and short. Mine is uk.linkedin.com/in/adamgray

 **brilliant** tip

Not everyone wants to just read what you say, so try to add some more varied content to your LinkedIn profile – videos, images, presentations ... they will all help add a little bit of zing!

The next few points are the dynamic bit. This is the part of your relationship with LinkedIn that will form your ongoing commitment. This is where you will be having conversations, being noticed and forging relationships.

brilliant tip

Although this part of your LinkedIn profile is fairly static, you should still regularly update elements of it to reflect what you're doing and any new skills you have gained.

4 Groups

At the end of 2012 there were a staggering 1,477,950 groups on LinkedIn. The largest of these has well over 1 million members, the smallest has just 1 member: the person who started it.

Groups are basically meeting places where people who have a shared interest or goal can come together and have discussions, share ideas and generally interact in an environment where they don't need to dumb down. For most individuals (and businesses) there are benefits to be gained from joining groups or even starting a group.

> there are benefits to be gained from joining groups or even starting a group

The only limitation is that each person can join only a maximum of 50 groups. This should be more than enough for most people though!

Most groups (although not all) are 'open' groups, meaning you can just click the 'join' button and you're in. Some, however, pass your request to join to a 'moderator', usually the person who started the group, who assesses your application. Once you have successfully joined a group you will be able to see all the members of the group, read all existing discussion threads, make comments and even start a new discussion topic (or poll) if desired.

Generally I would suggest exercising caution when first join-ing any group. Invest a little bit of time in watching discussions develop before just plunging straight in. Remember the old adage, 'you can only make a first impression once'!

Try to identify who are the main 'movers and shakers', those people who are plugged in to large communities and are most active within the group and start to have a conversation with them.

It goes without saying (but I'll say it anyway) that it is crucial you are absolutely certain of your facts – any mistakes you make are on a public stage and you possibly won't be the only expert from your industry as a member in the group.

Generally there are two types of group that you may be interested in joining, for very different reasons.

- *Your industry groups.* If you are a thought leader within your industry or are simply keen to keep up with the latest thinking, joining some industry groups may be a huge time-saving resource. You can simply 'tune in' and see what everyone is saying about the key industry issues – all in one place. So you should probably consider your industry groups primarily as a learning resource. Although not impossible, it is unlikely that you will win new business from groups centred on your own industry. This is because your clients are too busy thinking about their industries to worry about yours.

- *Groups inhabited by your clients.* They too, will be discussing their industry issues. It may be a great intelligence-gathering tool to discover what troubles your clients, but, with luck, you may also see opportunities when clients air specific issues that you may be able to solve. Over time this will possibly become an important new business tool.

5 Newsfeed

This is what social media is all about. This newsfeed shows what's going on in your network and, in one form or another, you will see this on pretty much every social media network. Generally you will find the newest news at the top and the oldest news at the bottom, while attached to each piece of news/update is a photo or some sort of visual identifier so you can easily spot the people who have managed to engage you. On LinkedIn this contains all sorts of information, some more useful than others. Who's connected to whom, who's said what, who's updated his or her profile and various other pieces of information. Every time you log in to LinkedIn this will be the first thing that you see and it's always worth investing a few minutes scanning down a few pages to see if anything catches your eye. It may be that someone has changed jobs, been promoted or shared a piece of valuable news ... whatever it is, it may be worthy of a comment. The more you comment on other people's updates, the more they will see you as 'one of the good guys' and the more they will be likely to read and comment when *you* post an update.

As you start to use LinkedIn in a more structured way, you'll need to consider how much of your time you spend reading what others are doing. Generally I would suggest the more the better (within reason). I say this because people generally don't care about you, they're too busy worrying about themselves, so when you post an update about the fact that you've won a new client or have delivered a fantastic presentation they probably won't engage too much with it, but when you comment on one of their updates ... they will.

So, the more that you see what other people are doing, the more likely you are to find something you can comment on. Flattery, as you know, will get you anywhere!

6 Apps

To underline the ever-changing nature of these social platforms, in between the second and third edits of the manuscript for this book, this section was going to be about apps for LinkedIn (little applications that you could install on your profile to enable you to import or show things drawn from other social platforms), but these have now been removed as a feature.

Most people used them for just one thing, though – to add multimedia content to their profiles, usually videos.

Now, however, it's far simpler: just edit your profile and at the top of each section is an 'add content' icon. Click this and you can simply paste in a URL/link to a huge selection of external content – video (not just YouTube and Vimeo but also BBC, CNN and many other approved content providers), presentations (including SlideShare and Prezi) and image sites such as Pinterest.

7 Contacts

Once you have started to make some connections with people, you will need to start to sort them into groups. For the first 100 or so connections just leaving them in a single list will be sufficient, but as you start to get up into the hundreds you will want to think about how you group similar people together. You do this with tags. By default your contacts are tagged based on the way you connected with them – colleagues, clients, friends, group members. You can change this (best to do this sooner rather than later) to something that better suits your needs.

The reason that you should invest a little bit of your time in tagging people as you connect to them is, you can use your LinkedIn address book as a simple email marketing tool. You can write an email and send it to either hand-picked individuals or entire portions of your contact list (up to a maximum of 50 in one go).

This is quite attractive as, if you are connected to people on LinkedIn, they have already in effect 'approved' you, so they are much more likely to read a message you send them. Also, because the mail is dealt with by LinkedIn it isn't subject to the same screening as your corporate email might be, so it's a lot more likely to get to its destination.

When you send a bulk mailing, it is properly merged so it looks as though it has arrived as a personal note rather than a mailing, which again helps to maximise the number of people who actually read it.

brilliant tip

Clients, prospects, friends, local businesses ... whatever you choose to use, these tags are not seen by the people, which is just as well because I have a tag called 'not interested' for people I don't want to have too much conversation with!

Remember, as a connection, you are in a privileged position. Make sure you don't abuse it by spamming people – if you do, you may find that the people you're doing it to disconnect from you or, worse still, if you get reported to LinkedIn too many times, you may get banned from the network (which would mean starting again from scratch).

8 Jobs

Often LinkedIn is highlighted as one of the best tools for recruitment. Currently approximately 80 per cent of top executive vacancies in the US are filled via LinkedIn (according to LinkedIn!) and this is easy to believe.

Your profile page (if filled out properly) will provide a recruiter with all the information needed to identify if you are a likely candidate. With information such as employment history, personal statement (summary), testimonials (references) and experience, everything that prospective employers need to know is at their fingertips.

This is a really good place to start to fill a vacancy. If you want to move on or have lost your job, there is also the opportunity for you to take a more proactive role by searching for job vacancies that have been posted, then refining by industry, location and even how connected you are to the person who posted the job opportunity.

When you look at the job vacancy you can see all the relevant information, including, interestingly, how many people in total have applied for the job through LinkedIn.

Then, if you like the look of it, you can apply with a single click. You have the opportunity to add a covering letter and/ or résumé to add a degree of personalisation, although much of this will, of course, be covered in your profile anyway.

9 Inbox

Your inbox operates in much the same way as your Outlook Inbox does. Mail/messages arrive and are flagged as 'unread' – opening them will mark them as read. You can then respond, delete, forward or archive the message as appropriate. Your inbox has two tabs, messages and invitations, which are pretty self-explanatory.

For each of these two tabs there are four links (on the left) – inbox, sent, archived and trash. This enables you to keep track of which messages you've sent to whom and (as messages quickly mount up), if you delete messages once they've been replied to and actioned, it's quite a good tool for keeping track of who you need to talk to within LinkedIn.

 **tip**

Remember that a personal message is far more compelling than a general broadcast. Make use of the network you're building by talking directly to the people who are your contacts, but don't abuse this trust – make sure you only talk to them about things that you think they'll be genuinely interested in.

Network size

LinkedIn has a clear policy – 'You should only connect with people you know well' – which, while encouraging people to keep a tight network, in my opinion goes against that ethos of networking. I believe you need to have a reasonably big network, not massive, but reasonably big, so I personally think it's a good idea to connect to new and interesting people whether you know them or not.

Now, this is an important point – you must have an *engaged* network. Your network can be as big as you like as long as you know who people are and why you're connected to them. LinkedIn seems to me to be like an online metaphor for a 'chamber of commerce' or other large networking event. Part of the reason for going is to meet new people. If someone walks up to you and holds out a hand, you can either shake hands and have a chat or you can turn round and walk away. I would suggest that the person is more likely to be of benefit to you (and you to him or her) if the two of you connect and get to know one another.

> if you spot people you would like to connect to, then connect to them

I am not suggesting that you go around connecting to people willy-nilly just to get a large network, because that is a waste of time, but if you spot people you would like to connect to, then connect to them.

However, 'I'd like to add you to my professional network on LinkedIn' is the standard line that accompanies a connection request. I would change this to something that's more personal. Whenever I connect to someone I always write something funny if it's someone I know and something charming if it isn't. Let's be honest, you're more likely to get someone to accept your request if you write 'I was browsing around LinkedIn and came across your profile and it looks really interesting. I would like to connect with you if that's OK to keep in touch because I might have an opportunity for you with a new client at some point. Thanks, Adam' than if you just use the standard line, which looks like you haven't given the connection any thought whatsoever.

Note: if you get too many 'I don't know this person' flags, LinkedIn will give you a warning ... then may close your account so it's important to get the people you send an invitation to to say 'yes'.

Because LinkedIn is a global network I wouldn't just think about connecting to people in your local business community ... go global. However, what you certainly don't want is 190 million connections as this would be unmanageable. So connect to people at a similar level within the business world. If you are a senior manager, there's probably less value in connecting with an office junior than there is with another manager.

So remember that what you need is a network of people who are of a broadly similar seniority to you (or, better still, above) as they are more likely to be able to help and connect you.

By connecting to these people you are opening a line of communication that wasn't there previously and they are potentially trusting you with their time – don't abuse this trust.

As I said earlier, *engaged* is the important thing to remember. Having 5,000 connections you haven't invested any time in talking to is likely to be of less value to you than 500 people who all really rate and respect you. So when you've connected, listen to what they say, comment and begin a dialogue.

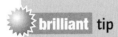 **tip**

Make sure that you give some thought to how big your network needs to be. Too small and you haven't got enough people to talk to, but too big and you can't keep track of all the people there and can't have close enough relationships with them to generate any business. How big the network should be will probably depend on how much time you can invest in LinkedIn.

Protocol

Outside of the 'Only connect with people you know well', LinkedIn doesn't really give much steer in terms of what is appropriate and, more importantly, what works. This, though, is the easy bit.

You need to act on LinkedIn exactly as you would in a face-to-face networking environment. Be charming, be helpful, try not to say too many things you'll regret later and *don't sell*. If you follow these basic principles, you won't go far wrong.

> try not to say too many things you'll regret later, and *don't sell*

The power of search

Along the top bar in LinkedIn is a search box. A dropdown menu within the box enables you to search for people, companies, groups, jobs and more. Typing into this box searches as you type and immediately presents the closest people to you in your network first (1st-level connections, then 2nd-level, then 3rd, etc.). To the right of this box is a small 'advanced' link. Clicking this will take you to a much more sophisticated search tool.

Depending on what level of account you have (free, business, business plus or executive), certain features may be available or not.

Assuming that you have access to all the search facilities, you can limit search results based on distance from a specific post-code, company size and seniority levels in addition to keywords and name. As LinkedIn continues to grow this will become more and more important (for example, on 12 December 2012 searching for Adam Gray delivered 550 results and David Smith more than 28,000 results!)

If you search for a keyword, perhaps within a specific geographical area or industry, you will be delivered a number of results (sorted by closeness to you). Clicking on one of the results will show their profile. On the right side of their profile you will see a box titled, 'How you're connected to X' – this is a very powerful feature as it shows the person (or people) who connect you to this new person. For example, if you want to meet me, you can see that we might well be connected by a person who is present in both of our networks. If this is the case it's much better to ask for an introduction than approach someone cold. At the time of writing, LinkedIn is the only network that exposes this relationship path beyond your immediate connections, which could be really useful for you in bringing in new business/clients.

Planning a LinkedIn strategy

Because LinkedIn has a message/email system where you can segment your connections, it can in part function as a mini customer relationship management (CRM) and email marketing system. Because of its great CV and job facilities it's a potential recruitment system; because of its timeline it's a potential newsfeed and general intelligence-gathering tool. It really is a complete ecosystem in itself, but first and foremost it is a networking tool. So, for this reason it's probably worth spending a little time considering exactly how LinkedIn could be used within your business.

When implementing a business-wide LinkedIn strategy there are two elements that will need to be created and administered centrally.

- *The company profile.* A well-written, keyword-rich (brief) description of what the company does is a vital tool to tie together the company message and (as things currently stand with Google rules) is replicated across all the employees' personal profiles.

- *Training.* At the simplest level it is vital that staff who work within the same business all link to the company profile as their current employment (obvious, but a frequent mistake). It's important that the staff also set up the website links from their profiles to the company website (or better still, specific pages) in the most effective way. Perhaps most importantly, staff should understand why they are using LinkedIn and how easy it is to use it effectively and that being themselves (usually!) is the most valuable asset they can bring to their LinkedIn presence.

As the staff who will be using LinkedIn become more comfortable and confident with it, they will probably need it to do more, understanding how to identify prospects and stimulate conversations within groups to make themselves the centre of attention.

Understanding what's important to your business and communicating it are not the same thing, so it's important to tell staff what they need to do and why. If you're in a smaller business it's important to write down what you're going to do, why and the steps to get there … otherwise it simply won't get done.

Research

Whether you're going to a job interview or a pitch, LinkedIn is a fantastic resource to gather information about both the company and the people within it. You can easily see where people have worked before; you can usually see who they're connected to and certainly how they're separated from you. This could prove invaluable intelligence if one of your friends or contacts knows them and is able to give you a little insight on them.

However, it is worth remembering that if you view someone's profile, they will get a notification about this (unless you adjust your settings – see the following section).

Settings

This is the nerve centre and controls how often you receive notifications from LinkedIn and for what, your email preferences and what information people see when you've viewed their profile.

This last point is pretty important. Usually (and the default setting) it is that people whose profile you've viewed can see that it's you. This is generally a good thing as social networking is based on openness. However, sometimes you may want to conduct covert research (or just have a look and see how that ex-boss is doing) and you'd rather they didn't know that you've seen them. In this case, amend your 'select what others see when you've viewed their profile' settings and make sure that it's 'totally anonymous'. Make sure when you've finished that you set it back to the recommended setting, otherwise you won't be able to access some of the insights into who's viewed your profile.

Openness

... is a good thing. The basic reason that people should be joining LinkedIn (and any other online network) is for the same reason that they should be going to a real-life networking meeting: to meet people. The more open you are to meeting new people, the more likely you are to meet someone interesting.

Paid or not

Generally I would suggest that a free subscription is perfectly adequate to begin with. It offers all the basic facilities, just in a cut-down form. The biggest reason for upgrading your account that I come across is people aren't getting a long enough list of search results. A free account gives you 100 search results for any given search, which seems plenty, but, as your network grows, you could easily arrive at the point where searches deliver only people you are connected to (no matter how you cut the results). Upgrading to the first of the paid accounts gives 300.

Other tools

LinkedIn has a number of funky hidden tools such as LinkedIn Labs, where you can produce an 'InMap' of your network. While this has no obvious use, it's quite good fun and a visual representation of how your network looks, with all of the connections between people. It is a great reminder of the power that your network has. Figure 7.1 is an InMap of a personal network. Every dot is one of the connections and every line is a relationship between two of the dots.

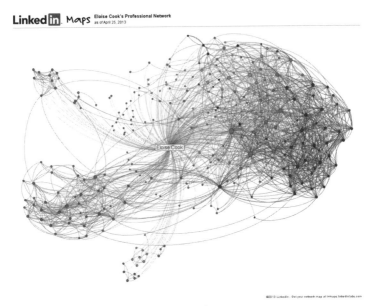

Figure 7.1 InMap of a LinkedIn network

The ramifications of this may not be immediately apparent, but they are as follows.

- It's amazing how many of the people in your network know the same people you know – so if you can get some of these people to talk about you in a positive way, it adds up to quite a lot of noise.

- A network is an incredibly complex system and without the aid of LinkedIn you would never be able to see how your connections fit together.

- You can see some of the people within the network are obviously more connected (and therefore more valuable) than others – and consequently should demand more of your time and effort.

brilliant recap

- LinkedIn is the biggest business network and is a great tool for prospective employers, clients and partners to check out what you've done and what people think of you.

- Having a great profile, though, is not enough. To get the best from LinkedIn you need to be active in both updates to your status and your activity in groups.

- LinkedIn is a complete business sales and marketing platform. It offers research tools, introduction tools, meeting places and even a mini CRM system to keep track of all your contacts, but it's just one part of the social media sphere.

CHAPTER 8

Facebook

What is it?

Facebook is the biggest network there is. Currently it has just over 1 billion members and for this reason alone it is arguably the most important network for both individuals and businesses.

brilliant tip

Over half of the UK population has a Facebook account and the number continues to grow, but this isn't the only reason you should take notice of it. It is one of the 'stickiest' sites on the internet – meaning that when people come to Facebook they tend to stay for a long time, so they're not just coming to comment on a photo. Statistics produced by Hubspot show that a staggering 1 in 8 minutes spent online is spent on Facebook, so clearly there's a lot of opportunity to engage people on this platform.

How does it work?

It's like a virtual pub. There are lots of people there and they hang around chatting to each other in groups. Sometimes people from one group introduce people to another, but it's all pretty relaxed and a great way to create, renew and deepen friendships and relationships.

It isn't just people who are there. Brands are there too. So if you particularly like a brand – say Apple or Coke – you can 'like' this brand and then every time the brand updates its status or posts some information this shows up in your newsfeed.

As in the real world, you don't have to like everyone in this virtual pub. Even some of your friends you will like more than others … just like real life. Also, just like real life, if someone talks too much about themselves, doesn't ever listen or lies … people tend to like them less.

What are the benefits?

The reason this is so important is that if you personally (or your brand) can become part of your prospects' friendship group they will understandably develop positive feelings towards you and with luck find it very difficult to shop elsewhere.

Like LinkedIn, Facebook has a huge number of features and facilities, some of which seem a bit baffling at first glance. So, as with LinkedIn, I will cover all the main ones, along with how this can benefit you and how to get the feature working.

To begin with it's worth outlining that there are two types of page that you can visit on Facebook – personal and business. Then there is a series of features, tabs and applications that will run on each of these.

brilliant tip

As with LinkedIn, getting going with a Facebook business page can seem a little daunting, so here's the simple step-by-step guide, even if you do nothing else after that.

1   Sign up.

2   Complete your information section (nicely written but not too long).

> 3 For the first fortnight add at least one status update/wall post every day.
> 4 Invite everyone you know to 'like' your page.
> 5 If someone comments on a post, make sure you comment back.

So how do I sign up?

1 Personal profile

This is your own personal account. You must have one of these in order to set up a business page (as the two accounts are tied together). Your personal profile contains all the things about you – generally your photo, your friends (and the things you 'like'), what you're doing, some photos, some general info – and it is the place where you can post personal things and engage in personal conversations with people.

It's important to position Facebook in a place where you are comfortable that you have struck a balance between letting nobody in and letting everybody in (up to a maximum of 5,000 friends!)

Your Facebook personal page lets you talk to a large number of people about what you're doing and allows them to comment back in real time. It is, I suppose, the real-time equivalent of those photocopied sheets some people include in their Christmas cards that tell you all about what their families have done for the last 12 months. Clearly the big advantage with Facebook is that if you tell everyone that you've just become an aunt for the first time they can congratulate you before it's forgotten!

Personally I have a mixture of my real friends and my acquaintances within my 'friends' on Facebook. These are people I don't mind sharing stuff with and people whose company I enjoy and might typically go out to dinner with and I think I have the balance about right. This balance is such that it enables me to share some personal stuff, but nothing more than I might talk about when spending face-to-face time with the person. I certainly wouldn't talk about anything that would unduly embarrass me if it got into the public domain. This is, I suppose, a golden rule. *Never* write anything on your profile (business or personal) on *any* social network that might be damaging if it were seen by everyone, because, believe me, if it is embarrassing, it will get shared – that's human nature!

Your personal profile is a place where people can get to know the *real* you. In my opinion this can be clients and prospects you get on really well with as well as personal friends.

> your personal profile is a place where people can get to know the *real* you

The litmus test for whether or not I connect with someone is, 'Would I like you to be my friend?' rather than 'Are you my friend?' because, as with face-to-face networking, you have to give people a chance. After all, you can always unfriend them if things don't work out!

The more you manage to draw people into your circle of friends, the more they'll get to know you and like you, then the more chance there will be for you to do business together.

I wouldn't use a Facebook personal profile to promote your business, other than you might mention something that happened at work you're very pleased with as you would down at the pub. The place to promote your business is via Facebook 'business' pages.

Friends
Facebook is, in my opinion, the best way there is to keep in touch with far-flung (and not so far-flung) friends. Although most people have more *friends* than they have *close friends* these close friends are the people they tend to invest the most time in,

rightly so. The problem is that it's difficult to really get to know a large group of people because it simply takes so much time. Facebook is, for many people, the answer. It enables you to see what all of your friends are doing and comment/chat with them (and better still, their friends). It is a great online metaphor for being at a party. You can see someone else chatting to one of your friends, you can start to chat to them too, and if you hit it off you can become one of their friends.

As I've said, the word 'friend' can be a bit misleading. Online friends are not necessarily people you would want to come and stay with you for the weekend or people you'd happily lend money to, but then neither are people you've just met at a party.

The interesting thing is that, just like those people you meet at a party, if you keep chatting and get to know them, eventually they may become close friends. This is what Facebook enables and I believe passionately that this is a good thing.

Apps

Within the Facebook ecosystem there are many apps. These are little programs (or plug-ins) that you can add to your profile to enable additional features. These might be apps such as Skype that allow you to talk to your friends straight from Facebook or they might be games or news apps. Generally these apps will ask you to grant them access to some of your data and to be able to write on your wall. Always exercise caution when allowing an app to write on your wall because you are potentially allowing it to share personal information with all your friends or (in some cases) it might be a virus or spamming app that might write things in such a way everybody you are connected to thinks you have written them.

> exercise caution when allowing an app to write on your wall

In reality, I question how damaging these things can be to your reputation and consider them mostly as the Facebook equivalent of gossip … people like to hear it but usually don't believe it.

Games

There are various very popular games on Facebook. FarmVille and Mafia Wars spring to mind as two of the main ones. Facebook games run as apps on your profile and often they post to your timeline to tell your friends when you reach key milestones on the game. This is great as it gives your friends the opportunity to join in the fun. However, if everyone plays these games then you can be in a situation where everyone's timeline fills up with game notifications rather than items that you actually engage with.

At some point Facebook will need to find a way of limiting this posting frequency as this can make the Facebook experience rather dull for everyone concerned.

Comments

This is what social media is all about. It's all very well posting updates and hoping that people read them, but when people actually make comments (or click the 'like' button) you know you're starting to do something right. It is this interaction that both proves people are engaging and introduces social leverage, the spreading of your name and message beyond your immediate network.

It is worth remembering that people say bad as well as good things, so you must always police what's said on every social network to ensure the good is spreading and the bad isn't.

Growing your network

As with LinkedIn, your network has greater value for you as it gets larger. If you have a network of just 20 people, there is far less chance of 1 of these people knowing someone who needs your product or service than if you have a network of 100.

Protocols

It seems to me that there are some people on Facebook who treat it as if it were a competitive sport. Their goal seems to be to have as many friends as they can get. However, there has been a significant amount of study of this and Dunbar's Number (named after the primatologist Robin Dunbar) says that the 'maximum number of people with whom a person can maintain a stable social relationship' is between 120 and 230 (usually quoted at 150 for ease). The key thing is, the fewer closer friends will usually yield a greater benefit for you than a larger number of people you know less well.

However, Facebook has made provision for this by creating business pages. Business pages have many of the same features as personal pages, but have no size limits as to how many 'likes or fans' (the business equivalent of friends) you can have.

Generally speaking, most of the behaviour that you should be exhibiting on Facebook should really mirror your behaviour in the real world. Don't say unpleasant things about others because these things have a nasty way of biting you on the backside. Often things that are said to a closed group of friends find a way of leaking out (either through deliberate further sharing or lax security settings) and making it into the public domain. So don't ever write something you wouldn't want to be associated with you ... *ever.*

Unfriending

On Facebook, if you have fallen out with a friend (now an ex-friend) or you have got to know someone a bit better through interacting with them and you're not liking what you've seen, you can simply 'unfriend' them. I would suggest that you use this fearlessly and often. In my experience how nice a place Facebook is is directly proportional to how much you like the people around you (a bit like real life).

People have a habit of annoying each other when they spend time together, and Facebook is no different, but for some reason unfriending is viewed by some as a terrible action to take. In my book it is the online equivalent of walking away from someone you don't like at a party ... better to walk away than thump them! The same is true on Facebook. Better to unfriend them than to say something you'll regret at a later stage.

If, of course, you have a change of heart later you can always friend them again.

Safety

From a personal perspective clearly you need to be careful with what you choose to share on any social platform. Always we like to think the best of people, but sometimes they have other agendas, so giving too many personal details or information about your movements could be a risk. Tread carefully. You can always change your security settings and make your profile and the information that you share either more or less secure as appropriate.

> you need to be careful with what you choose to share on any social platform

2 Business page

For business purposes, this is where you should really be focusing your efforts. A business page is different from a personal page because, unlike a personal page where you have to approve my friend request, here I can just 'like' you. So this part of Facebook is naturally open as a network. By default this page will also be indexable by Google (which is good), so an active business page with lots of content will also be a benefit to your search rankings.

Business pages offer significantly more possibilities for customisation and functionality than do personal pages. Here's why: with tabs on your Facebook page you can add a huge amount of content and functionality – photos, downloads, polls, you can even embed a version of your website (complete with navigation) in one of the tabs. This gives you the opportunity to make your Facebook page in some ways as much of a destination as your website.

Your Facebook page has some significant pros and cons, as opposed to your website, and it's probably a good idea to understand these in order to be able to work out how a Facebook presence can add to your digital marketing.

The biggest problem with a Facebook page, unlike your website, is that you have some significant constraints as to how you can make it look. It will always have a blue frame and a Facebook logo, it will be limited to (at the moment) 480 pixels in width and it currently makes your timeline the default tab that visitors hit. Ultimately, because your page is hosted on Facebook, you do not have totally free rein of the visitor experience and this limits how well you can reflect your brand in this environment.

However, Facebook does something your website can't ever do and I think that is one of the main attractions of investing some time and thought in Facebook as a marketing tool. It is an often-quoted fact that it takes people six encounters with an organisation before they're happy to buy, so what you need is a mechanism for people to have repeated contact with you. If you drive traffic to your website they will possibly look around a little bit and, if they like what they see, they may come back tomorrow or next week or next month or … never. The problem is that you are effectively outsourcing the development of your relationships to the visitors themselves, relying on chance and them remembering to come back.

With Facebook, if you encourage them to 'like' your page every time you post on to your timeline, it will show up in their NewsFeed. This is brilliant because it means that you can take control of how quickly your relationship with them develops. Perhaps you'll post something every week, perhaps twice a week, perhaps every day ... but whatever you choose, the speed at which the relationship with the person develops is within your control.

It still, of course, requires the visitor to 'like' your page, but this is a great deal easier than trying to get someone to give you their email address to put them on your database – they can 'unlike' your page at any time, so this means that there's less 'risk' for them.

Tabs

If you imagine that your Facebook page is, in fact, a website in its own right, then tabs are the pages within this site. You can add as much and whatever content you like to these different tabs. There is a huge number of precreated ones available from Facebook, such as 'likes' (showing who has liked the page), 'photos' (self-explanatory) and many others. There are also more specific developer-created tabs (many of which are free) that require you to like the developer's page to gain access to them. Then there are specific tabs that you (or your developer) can create. Really, the only limitation is your imagination!

Before you rush out and start adding tabs all over the place, remember the adage WIIFM (what's in it for me) – does a visitor really want to read and engage with the tabs that you think are a good idea? Are they adding value to the visitor? If not, remember that 'less is more'.

Apps

Generally speaking there are two types of application. Those that run within the Facebook ecosystem will generally be part of a business page and will allow specific functionality or features.

Typically you would 'host' an app on your business page (although it isn't usually hosted by Facebook itself), giving you greater access to your fans' data, but you would access an app through your personal profile.

Remember that Facebook is primarily a person-to-person relationship platform. It enables you to stay in touch with your friends. Business pages were created to give organisations the opportunity to engage with prospective customers in a social environment and to be able to target who they wanted to talk to based on the wealth of data that Facebook stores about each of us, compiled from our social behaviours.

The idea that as a business you can present your company to people who are married or in a relationship, who are university educated, who live within 15 miles of Milton Keynes and are company directors is a pretty exciting prospect. It is this ability to micro-target your message to people that has been the main revenue stream for Facebook for the last few years.

The addition of apps allows you to harness this data in a variety of ways. The most commonly seen is when, on signing up for the app, you grant it authority to write on your wall and to access your timeline. This means that at its simplest level the app that you've installed can tell all your friends when you are using it. You typically see this in Facebook games. 'Adam has just harvested his crops in FarmVille' could be something that might appear on your wall.

The reason this is powerful is that the app can repeatedly message your friends on your behalf, reinforcing in their minds that you play this game regularly. The conclusion that many would draw from this would be it's a good game and the action they might take as a result would be to sign up and play the game themselves.

This type of reinforcement doesn't work with everyone, but it works with many. This is how we see games that become fashionable spreading very quickly throughout the community – as people keep seeing more and more of their friends playing a game, eventually they think, 'Perhaps I should play this too'. This effect is called social proof and we see its effects in so many areas of life: changing fashions, choice of restaurant or bar, TV shows, even holiday destinations. Everyone's buying Product A, therefore perhaps I should buy one too.

The reason that this is an important behavioural trait to understand a little bit is, if you're going to install an app on your Facebook page, you need to understand what actions you're trying to stimulate and what benefit you are going to offer to get the app launched and to reach critical mass (critical mass is, in this instance, the point at which the weight of social proof is such that you no longer need to market your app/idea as it just continues to grow of its own accord).

Typically, an app may do something useful for the user, such as catalogue their friends' birthdays, and will be free to install and use. The benefit is that you never miss another birthday. The trade-off is that the app will be able to tell all your friends you want to log their birthday details and they should sign up for the app so you can do this. I imagine that they are planning to charge for this service at some point (or sell advertising through it), but for the moment it's free, as are most apps.

There are other, smarter, ways of leveraging the power of others' networks through the use of external apps, which we'll discuss in more detail in Part 3. Whenever you are either installing an app on your Facebook business page or commissioning a custom app, though, consider (as seems to have become a bit of a theme for this book) whether you are producing something your audience wants or something you want.

If you are going to invest the time and trouble in creating an app from scratch, what are you trying to do? I would argue whether Facebook is the place to have a product configurator or a shopping cart – perhaps this would be a better place to focus on building the initial trust that precedes a sale rather than trying to actually close the sale. Use Facebook as a

> use Facebook as a conduit to enable a conversation to develop with your fans

conduit to enable a conversation to develop with your fans, so that they can get to know you and your brand a little bit. Then gradually move them towards your website, which should always be the focus of your online presence and is a place where you are in total control of the experience visitors have when they arrive.

Groups

As with LinkedIn, you can create groups on Facebook. As on LinkedIn, these groups are places where like-minded people can get together and discuss things and, like LinkedIn, you can have an open or a closed group.

As Facebook says, 'Have things you only want to share with a small group of people? Just create a group, add friends and start sharing. Once you have your group, you can post updates, poll the group, chat with everyone at once and more. Groups let you share things with the people who will care about them most. By creating a group for each of the important parts of your life – family, teammates, co-workers – you decide who sees what you share.'

brilliant definition

Open
Anyone can see the group, who's in it and what they post.

Closed
Anyone can see the group and who's in it, but only members can see the posts.

Secret
Only members can see the group, who's in it and what the members post.

Fans/likes

They used to be fans … now they're likes (although they are often still referred to as fans). These are people (or rather personal accounts) who have 'liked' your business page. This is the main point of creating a business page and a crucial benefit that Facebook offers over and above a traditional website. Yes, that's right, Facebook does something very important that your website doesn't do.

Once people have liked your page they have effectively given you permission to talk to them when you want to. Every time you post something on your timeline, they see it – you are in charge of the rate at which you talk to your prospects.

> the trick is in getting the visitors to your Facebook page to 'like' it

So the trick is in getting the visitors to your Facebook page to 'like' it. You can either make it so compelling that they really *want* to like it or you can give them some sort of incentive – the choice is yours.

If you have loads of good content, regular updates that are both pertinent and enjoyable and manage to create a sense of

brilliant tip

- Relationships develop based in part on familiarity. With traditional online media building familiarity is at best hit and miss because it's up to viewers whether they come back or not.

- If, however, you 'like' my Facebook page then the amount of information I share with you is within my control.

- This means that I can touch you with my message as often as I want to, developing our relationship at the rate that I want to rather than relying on you.

community, then the number of 'likes' should steadily rise. However, if you've been following the different elements of social media as you've been working through the book, you (possibly) will already have started to see that keeping this content coming in is no mean feat. Social platforms are notoriously hungry for content. If you post a new article once every day that means you need to write 250 articles per year (assuming you don't do business stuff at weekends), which is a lot of work. It certainly is worth it in the long run, but to begin with this might seem like a mountain to climb.

There are other ways of growing your likes. The easiest is to buy them. I don't mean that you pay to have loads of people from the developing world 'like' your page, but you incentivise people to like it with a 'fangate'. A fangate is a barrier that precludes people from having access to some of your content before they have become fans of your page. The way you do this is by offering some incentive, perhaps a price reduction on a product or free entrance into some kind of competition, either of which would potentially work quite well in getting people to like you – but because of the transactional nature of the incentive they may well 'unlike' you as soon as they have received it. The better option would be to create some good content, perhaps a white paper or access to a client area that contains resources the visitor can use. This is fundamentally a better way to retain these likes because the incentive acts as a further sales tool for the business, giving people an opportunity to try your product or service.

With the fangate you can force people to 'like' you and, as we've discussed earlier, these likes (the conduit for you to have regular conversations) are one of the most important reasons for taking part in the social media arena.

Installing a fangate is fundamentally quite easy – you can either build one from scratch (using a developer, probably) or you can simply plug in a ready-made one. Googling 'Facebook Fangate' will give you some guidance on what's good when you're ready to do this yourself, but currently Wildfire, SocialAppsHQ and WIX produce nice, simple fangates that can be installed and configured in a matter of moments.

In most instances you simply install the app, then switch on the fangate in front of one of the tabs that you have within your profile. Typically the page that you're protecting could have a link to download a document or a JPEG image containing a code to receive a discount. In all of these instances there are free and premium versions of the product (the free one has the company's name and a link to its page/site) but these are pretty much the same from a functionality point of view.

The nice thing about this is that you can have a play around and see which of them works best for you before having to commit to any of them.

Photos

Because we live in such a visual world and one where a page of text, particularly delivered on a computer screen, is seen as rather dull, you certainly need to have some photographs on your business page. Some people like to read, others like pictures, but there's little doubt that everyone will take notice of a lovely, arresting image. So, interesting photos that are relevant to your business should be used frequently to both spruce things up and add another anchor point for visitors.

Perhaps you can photograph products that you have, staff having fun, other offices and areas you've visited, new events you've chanced upon during travels, celebrity visits to your office … if you give it a little bit of thought you can probably think of dozens of photo opportunities for you and the business. Don't waste them, because **you can probably think of dozens of photo opportunities for you and the business** building up a library of interesting and quirky shots will help potential clients to see you as an interesting and entertaining company rather than a bunch of dullards!

Once you have these interesting shots you can start to add them to your status updates and general posts. You can 'pin' them to your timeline (as it used to be called) – this is where you highlight the photograph to run full-width rather than just one column in your timeline. Varying the size of photos, giving prominence to the important or beautiful ones, is a really significant way of adding visual interest to both your photo albums and your timeline.

On the face of it you might not think that this is vital, but, remember, there are 1 billion people on Facebook. So, once again, you want to try and use as many tools as possible to make yourself stand out from your competitors.

Graph Search

In January 2013 Facebook launched an innovative feature called Graph Search. It is an internal Facebook search engine that lets you do a number of things which used to be quite fiddly, such as see all the photos you've been tagged in or look at all the posts you've commented on. This is great if you want to examine your levels of interaction either as an individual or as a business.

However, this new feature opens up a whole host of possibilities by turning the Facebook ecosystem into a search engine, but a very different sort of search engine from Google, Bing or Yahoo!

Traditionally you have used a search engine to deliver helpful results such as finding a plumber or the nearest Italian restaurant and, generally, search engines deliver results that are reasonably useful in this respect. However, most search engines have a method for grading their results and the SEO (Search Engine Optimisation) industry is based on getting your website as high in those search results as possible. This inevitably means that the top slots in search results are occupied by the organisations with the best SEO rather than the organisations closest to what you're looking for. Searching for 'that little Italian Bistro near Covent Garden' is as likely to bring up Pizza Hut as it is Guido's.

The other, perhaps more fundamental, problem with traditional search engines is that they are based on fact rather than opinion. Now bear with me for a moment here. If you're looking for something factual, such as 'the telephone number for Selfridges' or 'the closest station to Cheapside', traditional search engines are perfect because they deliver facts. If, however, you wanted to eat at 'the most popular restaurant among your friends' or go for 'the most interesting walk in your town', traditional search engines fail in a big way.

The reason they fail is that they don't know anything about you and your network of friends ... they don't even know who you are. All the results that are delivered are based on the information on the destination website, with the exception of customer reviews on Google Local, but even taking these into account you are every bit as likely to end up at a poor choice as at a good one. A couple going out for a good meal to celebrate their fiftieth wedding anniversary are likely to have different criteria for a nice time than a group of work colleagues going out on a Friday night for a bite to eat, even though both may have searched for 'Italian restaurant with live music and a bar'.

Facebook, because of its size, is uniquely placed to be able to curate comments and content from your network to deliver results that are right for you. The important bit here is that it's *your* network. People generally surround themselves with people like themselves – similar age, similar interests, similar outlook. Not exclusively, but usually. You just need to look at your own friends list on Facebook to see where the similarities lie. Knowing that several people in your friends network have been to 'Pedro's Pizza' and had a great time means that it's likely you will have a great time there too … because your friends have so much in common with you.

That's brilliant (assuming it works, of course) because the results being delivered are unique.

If you and I were both to search for the same thing using a traditional search engine, we would probably get pretty much the same results. Facebook used this analogy: 'In web search it's very often the case that if you do a search for Apple and I do a search for Apple we're basically going to get the same results. Maybe I'll get slightly more technical results based on Apple Inc. and maybe you'll care about the fruit a little bit more but they're not that different from each other. However, on Facebook, when we do the same searches we get completely different results because of the depth of personalisation that we do.'

So searching with Graph Search would deliver wildly different results. For example, you might be a keen iPhone user and often be talking about that, you may even have a friend who works in an Apple Store. I, meanwhile (really do), have a friend who owns a commercial orchard of 10,000 trees and grows apples for a living. Traditional web searches couldn't possibly know that. They couldn't know that I needed to buy some of Henry's Suffolk apples rather than want to find a place to buy a car charger for my phone.

It is this degree of personalisation of results that makes Graph Search potentially so innovative. Questions like, 'What film are my friends seeing at the moment?' or 'Should I go to venue X to see that new band?' become searches that deliver real value and, most importantly, the results are based on what people like you think rather than how much investment has been made in search marketing by the business.

Facebook says that until now it has typically been a tool for keeping in touch with people and places you already know, but now with Graph Search it can introduce you to people and places you perhaps *should* know (based on the friends you have and the things you do).

If it works as Facebook hopes that it will it could revolutionise searching and I think Google should be very worried indeed. It could usher in a new way of people collecting appropriate information from the web and, more importantly, from their own networks.

brilliant recap

Facebook is the most widely used social network there is and as a business you need to be there, not just because more than 1 billion people worldwide use it but because it gives you the chance to place your content, your brand in among family, friends, interests and brands that are really precious to people.

A business page on Facebook lets you have a searchable resource where people can find you and it leverages the power of social networks by letting your 'fans' promote you to their networks.

CHAPTER 9

Twitter

What is it?

Twitter is what's called a microblogging service. In 140 characters you can say and share whatever you want with a global audience. On Twitter you don't need to approve followers (although you can block troublesome ones). They just ... follow you.

Twitter now has more than 500 million users who currently send over 200 million tweets every day! With Twitter you can find, follow and learn about people from all over the world and they can learn about you.

How does it work?

Like most social networks, Twitter places all the updates from your network in a 'stream', with the newest at the top and the oldest at the bottom, and these brief snippets of information paint a picture of what people are discussing and thinking about *now*. This is arguably not the place to market your business, but it is a fantastic environment for a) discovering things and b) demonstrating that you have your finger 'on the pulse' of what's happening in the world.

What are the benefits?

Whenever I work with organisations I find it's Twitter that gives them the most trouble with understanding what it does and how it can be of use to them. 'How can I say what I want to say in 140 characters or fewer, particularly because I have such a complex and diverse product and service offering?' (144 characters!) Well, the truth is that Twitter is about sharing tiny soundbites of current information. The important bit here is 'current'.

> Twitter is about sharing tiny soundbites of current information

Increasingly the reported news in the press is being found via Twitter – people at the scene are sharing what's happening and news agencies are following up on this breaking news.

Now, while you might be thinking, 'That's not of any use to me personally', it isn't actually the case. Because of the way that search engines index web pages, they are likely to deliver the most popular rather than the most recent pages, so searching for the reason for a traffic jam will deliver results about what happened last week or last year rather than the actual traffic you're stuck in. Also, if people ask for help – 'I need a new accountant' or 'Where can I buy a new pair of Nikes?' – a web search very probably won't deliver what they're looking for.

However, a search on Twitter will. It's a fair bet that someone at the front of the traffic jam will have tweeted about what's causing it … and you are then in a position to know whether you should sit it out or look for an alternative route. A search for Nikes might also highlight that a local shop has got a 20 per cent sale, but has run out of size 8.

Of course, people don't just chat about buying Nikes (although that would be a pretty cool thing to hear if you owned a shoe shop) – they are asking their networks all sorts of questions and

 **example**

To demonstrate just what a powerful tool Twitter can be, it is shaping the behaviours of the TV-watching public. Up until about 18 months ago there had been a gradual decline in the number of people watching TV live, with viewers preferring instead to delay the start so that they could use Sky+ or Tivo to skip through the adverts. However, now people are having real-time conversations about events such as the Royal Wedding, the Olympics or *The X Factor* and to be part of these conversations you need to be there at the same time. Your friends (and friends you haven't yet made) are chattering all the time about TV, news and world events and you can plug into this at any time with Twitter.

sharing all sorts of valuable content. Clearly, it's not very likely that my behaviour will be shaped on the say so of these casual contacts. However, it can help.

Recently I needed to buy a new laptop. As I saw it I had three options – an 11in MacBook Air, a 13in MacBook Air or wait for the not yet announced 13in MacBook Pro with Retina display. I tweeted that I had this decision to make and had dozens of suggestions from my network. Clearly I wasn't going to do anything at all on the basis of what one single person said, but the aggregated feedback of everyone was actually pretty useful to me and did help shape my final decision.

That question could just as easily have been about finding a new finance company or choosing a new accountant and, while a number of people suggesting the same thing probably won't immediately make the sale, it very probably will help me compile a shortlist.

To use Twitter effectively there are a few things about the network that you need to know and a few terms you may need to understand.

The most important thing is that Twitter is an open network. Unlike LinkedIn and my personal Facebook page, on Twitter I don't have to send you a request that requires approval. I simply 'follow' you. In doing so you get a notification that I have started following you and I receive all your updates as you send them. If I am problematic then you can 'block' me from getting those updates, but otherwise by default I will get them.

It is worth noting that when you sign up for Twitter you will be given the option to 'protect your tweets' – I generally wouldn't suggest that this is a good idea. A great strength of Twitter is its open nature and trying to avoid this can only lead to it not really delivering value to you.

What is it for?

Obviously with only 140 characters per tweet it's going to be pretty difficult to share anything that helps position you as an expert with so little space in which to do it. However, what at first glance may appear a weakness is in fact Twitter's greatest strength.

The 140 characters means that you have to keep the message/ strapline short in order for it to fit. This means your followers can easily skim through quite a high volume of tweets in their timelines in order to find one that catches their eye.

> your followers can easily skim through quite a high volume of tweets in their timelines

Because they can see so many tweets, it is really important that you say something eye-catching for your followers. 'This is an article I read about how banking legislation is adding extra safeguards to how traders deal with the money markets' is probably not as eye-catching as 'The end of banking as we know it ... thankfully' or something equally punchy and interesting.

In order to be able to share content within an environment where you can use only 140 characters, you probably are going to want to familiarise yourself with a URL shortener, such as bit.ly, ow.ly or tiny url (there's quite some choice).

There are a couple of reasons for this:

1 If you want to include a link to www.microsoftstore.com/store/msuk/en_GB/home?WT.mc_id=MSCOM_HP_GB_Nav_BuyShop, there's actually not that much space for the message to tell me why I should click the link.

2 If you have an account (usually free) with one of the URL shorteners, you can start to get some statistics on who's clicking the links that you share and when they are clicking them (there's more on this in Chapter 14).

Retweets

This is a term you may have heard with regard to Twitter. A retweet is where someone (usually a follower of yours) shares your tweet with their followers. When this happens it's a fantastic opportunity for your message to spread far beyond your usual audience. As an example, assume that everyone using Twitter (including you) has 200 followers. If you send a tweet to your followers it gets 200 impressions – that is to say, there is a chance it will be seen by 200 people.

(If you advertise in a national newspaper with a circulation of 200,000 copies, and each of these may be read by an average of 1.5 people, your advert will receive 300,000 impressions, but be aware that this is not the same as how many people have actually read *your* ad.)

Now let's assume you've found a very good article *and* you've written a catchy teaser you've tweeted to everyone. If 2 per cent of people retweet this (that is to say, 'share it with their followers') and 2 per cent of their followers share with theirs, your ad will receive 4,200 impressions for your tweet.

Clearly, the number of retweets is directly related to the quality of what you share, but this is a very powerful mechanism. Also, as things get bigger, they also get a lot better for you – for example, if everyone has 500 followers and gets a 4 per cent retweet rate among followers and their followers, your tweet would be seen by a staggering 210,500 people.

Replies

When you send a tweet, people can reply to it in exactly the same way as they might to an email, except that it's available to the whole world to view. This is quite powerful because those exchanges can often be quite enlightening for the casual watcher. Typically a conversation (in default format) might look like this:

Me – 'It's just been confirmed that I shall be speaking at this year's Digital Bootcamp for the CiM'

Response – '@TheAdamGray – great, what is the confirmed date and venue?'

Me – '@JohnSmith – it will be at the University of Hertfordshire on 14 September … it starts at 09.30'

Response – '@TheAdamGray – cool, I'll try to be there – where can I get tickets?'

Me – '@JohnSmith – try **http://bit.ly/a3wTU2** *– I hope to see you there'*

Now, there is a major point to notice here. Because of the way that Twitter works, this conversation will only appear in the timelines of @JohnSmith, @TheAdamGray and anyone who follows both John and me. This is because each of the reply tweets *starts* with a username. Note, though, that this is *not* a private conversation – visiting either John's or my profile will show all the tweets in the conversation, they just won't appear on your timeline if you don't follow us both.

For the whole conversation to appear on the timelines of all of my followers I will need to modify each of my tweets so that it *doesn't* start with a username. Then the conversation would possibly look like this:

Me – 'It's just been confirmed that I shall be speaking at this year's Digital Bootcamp for the CiM'

Response – '@TheAdamGray – great, what is the confirmed date and venue?'

Me – 'It will be at the University of Hertfordshire on 14 September @JohnSmith and it starts at 09.30'

Response – '@TheAdamGray – cool, I'll try to be there – where can I get tickets?'

Me – 'try **http://bit.ly/a3wTU2** *– I hope to see you there @JohnSmith'*

Although the difference isn't huge it is significant.

You should try, though, to include the username in each tweet of the person you're in conversation with, so it is flagged up in their 'mentions' column so they don't miss it.

You might also notice that the last tweet has a shortened link in it – this is a way of saving space as the URL **http://bit.ly/ a3wTU2** in fact links to **www.GrayUK.com/events** (but would in fact be the same length irrespective of how long and convoluted the destination address is).

brilliant tip

Remember, to maximise the visibility of your tweets try not to start them with a username unless of course you're not bothered about the visibility of the tweet you're about to send.

Direct messages

As opposed to simply replying to someone you follow you can send them a direct message (assuming they follow you too). This is just like an email – direct messages between two people are visible only by the two parties involved. This is particularly useful as a tool to deal with any problems that might be being discussed in an otherwise open platform.

For example, if you had just completed a successful project for a new customer and wanted to tell everyone (although I'm not quite sure why they would be interested to hear it – remember WIIFM) and you posted a tweet saying, 'Delighted we've just completed our first project for Smith & Co – another satisfied customer!', that would tell everyone in your network a piece of information which reflects well on you. Assume, though, that you were being followed by an unhappy customer and she decided to reply to this, saying, 'I'm glad that this project worked out OK @fictionalexample because the last two projects for me have been awful ... I am *not happy*.'

At this point, you would probably want to continue this conversation to establish what the problem was and how you could rectify it, but you probably wouldn't want to do this in the public domain. So the direct message is a very handy tool for you. You can maintain the conversation with the customer on Twitter, a medium you know she is comfortable using (because you're having the conversation with her on it already), but you have moved the conversation out of the public domain and into a private situation where the customer can say whatever it is she wants but without it damaging your reputation or brand.

Assuming that you are able to deal with this customer's issue, it might be good to then move the conversation back into the public domain so anyone who was either following the conversation or discovered it later would be able to see a successful and satisfactory resolution to the customer's problem.

 **brilliant** tip

Keep positive comments and conversations in the public view for as long as possible; move problems and complaints offline as quickly as you can.

Hashtags

Twitter says, 'The # symbol, called a hashtag, is used to mark keywords or topics in a tweet.

Because so many tweets are sent about so many subjects, the sheer volume of information can be simply overwhelming. A staggering 200 million tweets are sent every day and because there are more than 500 million users it can become quite difficult to filter this mountain of information to find something useful. So the hashtag is a powerful tool for users of Twitter to be able to label a tweet so that it can be easily found. It enables tweeters to show that their tweets are related to a specific topic and it enables groups of tweeters to aggregate their tweets in one place.

> the hashtag is a powerful tool for users of Twitter

For a simple feature the hashtag is actually surprisingly difficult to describe. Before I show some examples of the hashtag in action, it's worth noting that Twitter says the hashtag 'was created organically by Twitter users' – this means that the feature was not launched by Twitter but adopted by Twitter because the users were already using it as a regular means of creating groups of tweets. This really shows the power of social media and open communities at work – one of the major social platforms creating new product features based on the behaviour of its users.

Imagine what this insight could do for your business. Perhaps your customers are asking for a different-coloured widget. Perhaps they need different sizes or materials. Perhaps your pricing is too high (or too low). What you can learn from listening to customers and prospects talk about your product or industry can be a very powerful tool to help shape a product or service that fits your customers' needs. More about this, though, in the section on R&D in Chapter 15.

Typically people use hashtags in three ways – to start group discussions, to join group discussions and to add interest to their tweets.

As I said at the beginning of the chapter, the use of Twitter is driving people to watch TV and other world events in real time (as opposed to using Sky+ or Tivo) and it is the hashtag that enables this massive shift in public behaviours to happen. During any major TV programme or world event, naturally people want to discuss what's happening and searching for #london2012, #royalwedding, #silverjubilee or even #canadiangrandprix will open up a whole world of conversations and fans of these events, all of whom are talking to their global audiences in real time about the events.

This has a number of effects. First, you can strike up a conversation (and relationship) with people you otherwise wouldn't meet – these are people who perhaps are totally outside your network and geographical region (or even country), but you share an interest/viewpoint. Second, you can be part of a bigger conversation than just that which takes place within your network. Third, with a bit of thought you can harness the power of these third-party conversations.

Imagine you have a stand at a trade exhibition and are demonstrating a new product or service. Places are strictly limited and a queue is starting to form. As the queue lengthens, people start to get annoyed – this is not good for your brand because you want people to make the association between your brand and speedy service, customer satisfaction, a generally happy experience. With Twitter you can tell people to follow the hashtag #adamsdemo and, by labelling your tweets, you can manage the flow of customers to the demos in real time.

'We're so busy that there's a 35-minute wait to see our great new product – leave it for a while before visiting us if you can #adamsdemo' (136 characters)

If, instead, things get a bit quiet, how about, 'We're showing an exciting new product demo every thirty minutes why not visit us on stand 327 at @socialmediaworld #SMW2012 #adamsdemo' (134 characters)

This tweet contains a number of elements that you will have noticed:

- *the message* – a concise comment about our half-hourly product demo – keep it short
- *our stand number* – so people know where to find us
- *the hashtag for the conference #SMW2012 (Social Media World 2012)* – so that any visitors to the conference hoping to find any seminars and events while they're there will find our message

- *the username of the conference* – @socialmediaworld – because we're hoping that if we mention them they might retweet us to their followers
- *the hashtag for Adam's Demo* – #adamsdemo

Clearly this is quite a niche use for Twitter, if a bit basic, but it helps to illustrate the real-time nature of the network and hopefully there will be ways that you can manage customer flow, announce promotions or share the good feelings your happy customers have.

brilliant tip

Hashtags offer a way of identifying and grouping tweets of similar content (or about a similar subject). Make sure you use hashtags if you're discussing something that has a wider audience than just your contacts.

Mentions

As I mentioned above (no pun intended), mentions are where a specific username is 'mentioned' in a tweet. Twitter logs these mentions and, through its user interface, flags these up to the account that has been mentioned. As things currently are (although this does change from time to time as Twitter updates its interface) any time that you're mentioned – by which I mean your username @theadamgray rather than your name 'Adam Gray' – when you log on to Twitter you will see a highlight under the '@ connect' tab at the top. Clicking this will take you to a page with both 'mentions' – every time someone references you in a tweet – and 'interactions' – the conversations you've been part of.

It is really important to keep on top of this and respond swiftly to mentions in an appropriate way. This is the Twitter equivalent of someone calling out your name – ignoring them is at best rude.

By default, because Twitter is an open network, everyone sees everything.

Anyone who follows your Twitter account will see everything you write, unless a) you start the tweet with a username (as mentioned above), b) you protect your tweets, meaning that you have a closed account (rather defeats the object of joining twitter) or c) you have sent/received a direct message.

Caution: as with every other social (or any) form of communication, be careful what you say. Twitter history is littered with comments that have been damaging to individuals/organisations because they haven't thought through the possible effects of the comment being taken out of context. Remember that when you send a tweet you are writing down a comment and this can be shared with a global audience in a matter of moments, so always read it one more time before pressing 'send'.

brilliant tip

Make sure that if you want everyone in your network to see the conversation you don't start your tweet with the other person's username (@theadamgray), otherwise the comment will show up only in the streams of the people who follow both you and the other person in the conversation.

Growing your network

Much of the use of social media is really just common sense. Many of the social networks have the same (or very similar) dynamics and growing your network is the same on Twitter as it is on any other social network.

The value that you can get from your network is directly proportional to how engaged your network is (the important bit here is 'engaged') – the more the better. However, your network needs to be listening to what you're saying.

your network needs to be listening to what you're saying

The best way to encourage someone to follow you on Twitter is to follow them … then say some nice things about the tweets that they're sending.

For example, 'Really good article @TheAdamGray – thanks for sharing, do you think that this holds true for businesses of all sizes?'

This approach works because:

- you have mentioned my name so it has been flagged up to me
- you have flattered me (you've said it was good and you've thanked me and you've also demonstrated that you want my opinion by asking me a question)
- you have constructed the tweet in such a way that all your followers have seen my name and there's the inference they should read the initial shared article themselves.

The reason that I will take notice of this tweet is because it's about the most important person in the world: me! Anyone who hears their name – particularly in the context of something good – will find it very difficult to ignore. Also, having read the tweet and seen some nice comments, it's likely that the sender will follow you, but, more importantly, actually _read_ what it is that you wrote and tweeted about.

Protocols

Generally what happens on the social networks should mirror what happens in real life – if someone is nice to you, perhaps by retweeting or mentioning your name, thank them for it. Be courteous at all times and *never* air your dirty laundry in public (no matter what the provocation). If somebody has a rant at another person or a business it reflects badly on everyone involved. If someone is having a rant at you, be calm, try to reason with the person and demonstrate your professionalism. If you get angry with them, people will assume that this is your usual behaviour. Is this something you want to be associated with?

#ff is short for FollowFriday. In 2009 people started to do this, it's a chance to mention to your followers anyone you think is worth them following as an appreciation of the fact that they share interesting content and make valuable comments. It's quite a nice thing to do as a reward for the efforts that some of your network have made, as recommendation will encourage others to check out that profile, generating more followers for them.

Trending

The most popular topics for discussion are said to be 'trending' – this is a sort of leaderboard for the most discussed topics. Typically, when you log in to Twitter you will be presented with a list of the highest-trending topics. This means that every one of the 500 million Twitter users will see that list of trending items when they visit Twitter.com (of course, many will use Twitter via other means – a mobile device, a management tool or through an automated feed), but even if only half of them visit the website directly that's still 250 million people who might want to check out the trending items.

Because of the way that trending topics are more visible than other general topics, there's an incentive to make your tweets part of a trending theme if you can. Clearly you aren't necessarily going to get more followers if lots of new people read your tweet, but there's a chance you will and it is through these 'chance encounters' that you will grow your reach and influence within the social space.

Therefore, commenting on (or better still starting) a trending topic is potentially very good for your profile. One way of doing this is by the use of #hashtags – this enables everyone who has a comment to make about a specific subject to use a common (and unique) label on their tweets.

 **brilliant** tip

Search for other Twitter users and key words/hashtags as often as possible to find interesting people to follow. Then try to engage them in conversation so that they notice you.

 **brilliant** recap

- Twitter is all about *now*. Try to make your tweets as current as possible. Make sure that you keep them in the public domain (by being mindful of where you insert usernames) and hashtag them where appropriate.

- Always remember that content is the important thing, so make your tweets interesting, make them funny, make them controversial.

- Whatever you do, make them valuable enough that your followers want to retweet them and comment on them.

CHAPTER 10

Google+

What is it?

Google+ is Google's attempt at breaking into the social media platform marketplace. It's worth noting that it's not Google's first attempt (there was Google Buzz and Google Wave before this), but it has been its most successful venture in this space to date.

Now, depending on where you are in the world, you may find that Google+ has more or less visibility to you. In the US, Google+ has achieved a lot of traction – for many people it's their social media platform of choice. Other countries have been slower to get on board. Having said that, I believe Google+ has been the fastest-growing social network ever and in 12 months has moved from launch to having over 400 million users – which is truly staggering. Facebook may have more than twice as many users, but it's taken it eight years to get there.

Google+ is a bit like a cross between Facebook, Twitter and LinkedIn. One of the cornerstones of why it's great is that you can segment your audiences and share different content with each of them – perhaps family, colleagues, acquaintances. Each of these gets a different level of access to your personal/ professional information. The desktop and mobile interfaces are lovely and elegant. They allow you to manage the incoming content into different groups (perhaps home/work, for example) and seem to offer the opportunity to meet and greet new people, a bit like LinkedIn and Twitter, rather than just helping to develop existing relationships, as Facebook does.

But – and here's the big but – while everything about Google+ is good, and in a lot of ways better than existing networks, is there room for another network for sharing what you're doing with your friends and contacts in a newsfeed/stream? So the question that you and your business need to ask is: do you want to invest some time and effort getting to know and developing your own circles of contacts and relationships in a network that ultimately might go nowhere?

If the answer is 'no', that's understandable, particularly as there are plenty of other networks for you to begin to develop a presence on. If the answer is 'yes', then there's a fantastic opportunity for you to get first-mover advantage on your competitors. You can be first (well, 400 millionth actually) to use the network; you can develop your own style; and you can make your mistakes and faux pas when relatively few people will take notice.

Personally, I think it's a great opportunity, so here's how.

What's it for?

Google+ is a social network for sharing images, videos and text with groups of people. It delivers the content posted from the people you choose to follow in a colourful chronological timeline with the newest content at the top and the oldest at the bottom – nothing new there, of course. How Google+ differs, though, is that I can place each of the people I follow in a 'circle' to catalogue them – friends, colleagues, interesting people, industry experts, jokers. I can label these circles as whatever I want to help me organise them into streams that make sense to me.

This is brilliant because it encourages you to follow lots of people, therefore getting varied and fresh content, because you can dip in and out of the circles as you fancy. I check out 'interesting people' every day, but I only look at 'jokers' to get some funny stuff to talk about when I'm going out with friends.

> you can dip in and out of the circles as you fancy

This is the fundamental difference between Google+ and the other networks. It enables you to organise the people you follow in a way that suits you and the way you want to organise your content.

It doesn't end there. Not only can you catalogue the people you follow into circles so you can organise your incoming content but you can also be selective about what you share with whom. You can share anything you like with your 'followers' as a whole, but then you can group followers into a more selective series of lists (again called circles). So, for example, you might have a circle for your family and friends, a circle for your colleagues, a circle for prospective clients and a circle for existing clients. Clearly, different groups of people may have different interests and certainly there would be different types of content that you would be comfortable sharing within each of these groups. From this perspective, Google+ has some unique attributes, which make it a very powerful tool to use … and a very comfortable one as well. You can share business content with your 'business' circles, you can share friends' content with your 'friends' circles and you can share more general positioning content with your 'leads and contacts' circles, all from within the same network, whereas previously you would have had to share some of the content through LinkedIn, some through Facebook and some through Twitter.

Perhaps, though, from a 'How can this help my business?' perspective, you should consider what Google's primary function is: doing searches.

In most territories Google holds more than 50 per cent of the search marketplace. In some territories it commands over 90 per cent. Understandably Google+ is helping Google shape its search results. That doesn't mean it's distorting results to favour Google+ users, but with such a vast in-house data resource, naturally Google is using this to help determine what it is you're actually looking for. So, as a result of this, a Google+ page will probably do far more to help you rise up the search rankings than a similar Facebook page might. I think it's pretty inevitable that Google+ is going to become a major cornerstone of every business' online marketing strategy in the future.

Google+ includes a neat little feature called +1. This is, if you like, the Google+ equivalent of a Facebook 'like' or thumbs-ups, but unlike a 'like' (excuse the pun), the effect of which is limited to the Facebook ecosystem and, more precisely, your network within the ecosystem, with Google+ enough thumbs-ups mean that your post can become a 'trend-ing' topic. This is in much the same way as it might on Twitter if enough people are talking about it and retweeting it, and best of all, this positive endorsement that your post gets from all these +1s means Google will start to see it as important and feature it in appropriate search results.

> enough thumbs-ups mean that your post can become a 'trending' topic

This interconnectedness of social content and search content is very exciting for businesses that are able to take advantage of it.

Why is it important?

Google+ is going to be the next big thing (well, with 400 million users it's already a big thing), so there's a chance for you to get in at the beginning. In terms of operation, if you have any experience of Facebook particularly, but LinkedIn to a lesser extent, then you should be able to adapt to what Google+ offers pretty quickly.

As with any social network, Google+ will be hungry for content and one of the bigger challenges that you're going to have to overcome is to find stuff with which you can feed the network. However, as with other networks, much of this content will come from the network itself if you know where to look.

Certainly one of the difficulties I found in the early days was finding people I wanted to follow (much like when LinkedIn started) and, to a greater or lesser extent, I am still finding this to be the case. Fortunately, though, there are a few resources that are certainly worth visiting to point you at good content.

The first is FindPeopleOnPlus, an extensive listing of people and businesses with a presence on the network. They are catalogued into different categories and listed by numbers of followers, so this should be a good starting point. Once again, as with all the other networks, you should be keeping your eyes open for other people to follow (as this serendipity and randomness are part of the joy of using social networks). So when a person you're following references someone else's post or +1s something that you like, you should check out what else the original person has done … you never know what you might find!

> you should be keeping your eyes open for other people to follow

What should you do?

Most people these days have a Google account – perhaps for documents, perhaps for gmail, perhaps (and I hope so) for Analytics – and if you do, adding a G+ account is simply a case of logging in and clicking a button. If not, you probably should be signing up for a Google account anyway.

So once you've done that, open a G+ account and, as with all the other social networks, begin by filling out all the fields, giving information about who you are, what you do and where you live (all the privacy settings can be amended, but to begin with fill in everything if you can). All this information will be used by Google to make suggestions about stuff you might be interested in.

Have a look around for people within your network who are on Google+ and connect with them. Once you have done this, adjust your privacy settings to a level that you're more comfortable with.

brilliant recap

- Google+ is a new network, but already big and growing at a staggering rate. It's like the best bits of LinkedIn, Facebook and Twitter combined and it offers great integration with other things in your Google account, like YouTube and Blogger.

- Best of all, as part of the search giant, everything that you do or say on here will pay dividends in your search visibility. However, as a new network, it's unproven and you will be taking a gamble as to whether or not you can get any business benefit from it.

- So, if you're feeling adventurous this is your chance to be a real innovator in the social media space.

CHAPTER 11

YouTube

What is it?

YouTube is the largest video-sharing community in the world. It is a site where individuals (and companies) can upload videos into a public place where visitors can watch them. YouTube has become a great resource for everyone to find the answers on how to do everything from learning to juggle to repairing a computer. Also, because these answers are available in a video format it often makes understanding them a great deal easier than it might be if they were presented in written form.

How does it work?

YouTube offers a platform for users to upload and share short(ish) video clips that they have created. These clips can be named and tagged so that YouTube can catalogue them and offer appropriate content in its search results. These clips can be public or private and can be viewed either on the YouTube site or embedded in another website (such as your own website).

What are the benefits?

YouTube was started in 2005 and became very popular very quickly. It was bought the following year by Google (for $1.65 billion) and is now one of the most-visited sites on the internet.

In fact, the search function on YouTube is the world's second most-used search engine (after Google itself).

As of December 2012 YouTube statistics are truly staggering:

- 800 million unique visitors every month
- 4 billion hours of video watched each month
- 72 hours of video content uploaded every minute
- in 2011 there were over 1 trillion video views (that's 140 for every person on earth)
- 500 years of YouTube videos are watched every day on Facebook
- 700 YouTube videos are shared on Twitter every minute.

Clearly, in terms of being plugged into the world as a whole, YouTube is a pretty good place to be, but from a business perspective, the reason for being there is far more than just the access you get to a potentially huge audience.

Visibility

YouTube is not the only video-sharing platform out there. In fact, there are many of them. Some of these offer facilities that YouTube doesn't and some of them don't place the same restrictions about size of video or content that YouTube does. However, YouTube is the only video-sharing platform owned by Google. This means that, despite the fact Google is as impartial with its search results as it's possible to be, because they are part of the same business they view what's important (in terms of content) in the same way – so it's likely the way YouTube indexes its content is broadly similar to the way Google indexes it. For that reason most of the video which

> most of the videos which show up in Google's results will always come from YouTube

shows up in Google's results will come from YouTube. It is this added visibility that is one of the biggest pulls for using YouTube video.

Let me digress a little and explain. The science (or art) of search engine optimisation (SEO) is all about creating content to sit on each of your web pages that not only appeals to the visitor but also appeals to Google. When Google delivers search results for any given search term or phrase, it ranks those results based on a number of factors (which are always changing). Broadly these factors are these.

- *Relevance:* if I have searched for the phrase 'collectable Barbie dolls', is the page that Google has suggested really about collectable Barbie dolls or is it just a page where the phrase 'collectable Barbie dolls' appears? The more obviously the page relates to the search phrase, the more likely Google is to rank it highly. This is why successful SEO requires a time investment in keyword analysis to ensure that pages are seen for the right terms and terms for which competition is relatively low.

- *Popularity:* how many links are there pointing at the page? Google thinks (and with some justification) that if there's a page with no links pointing at it, it's likely not to be as good as a page which has loads of links to it from all over the internet. This is why SEO requires a certain amount of 'off-page' optimisation, forging partnerships with other sites and with referrers from all over the internet.

- *Age:* if the page is very old (or, rather, hasn't been changed for a long time), it's likely to be less interesting than a very dynamic and recently updated page. This is in part why so many websites now have a blog. The nature of a blog and the fact that it is regularly updated means this a vital element for making any website visible.

- *History*: when Google has shown a link to your page to people in the past, have they actually clicked it? If so, then there's a higher chance that it's answering the query people have had than if it isn't getting clicked.

All of these factors are mixed together in various proportions, according to Google's search algorithm, to deliver the most appropriate results for any search that you may conduct.

I'm sure you will agree that SEO is a pretty complicated process. It is time-consuming if you do it yourself and costly if you get someone else to do it. (I would exercise caution when someone phones and says, 'I can get you on the first page of Google results for £50' because they can't in any meaningful way. For me to get on the first page of results for 'Adam Gray Social Media' is easy because I'm the only Adam Gray who specialises in social media – *and* it's not really of much use because by the time someone searches for 'Adam Gray Social Media' they already know who I am! For me to get on the first page of results for 'Social Media Expert UK' is very difficult indeed. I'm not saying it isn't worth the investment, because it almost certainly is, but it isn't cheap and it is an ongoing investment rather than a 'do it and forget it' investment.

> it is an ongoing investment rather than a 'do it and forget it' investment

So, because there's so much competition for the 'first page real estate' of Google, it's very difficult to get there (or at least to get there for things that people are actually looking for). However, there's a lot less competition for the slots that Google allocates for the top videos.

Embedding

YouTube is a very flexible platform. Its open nature means that you can host your videos on YouTube and then embed

 **tip**

Creating the video and tagging it with the keywords that you want to be found for could be an easier way to get first-page visibility in the short term and certainly a very valuable by-product of work that you're probably going to be doing anyway.

them in other places. (Embedding is basically creating a viewing window in another location, through which your video will play – it sounds difficult but it usually takes just a single click to set it up.) The advantages of this are that YouTube handles the bandwidth and hosting of the video, which is important if you become popular and lots of people start to view your content. For example, Stephen Fry is one of the most popular Twitter users in the UK, with over 5.25 million followers, many of whom read and action everything he says. If he were to mention your website it would almost certainly crash as traffic would increase from perhaps 1,000 visitors each month to 250,000 visitors an hour. If you host the videos yourself you always have this traffic problem – and missing an opportunity like that would be a great shame.

Also, typically, the hosting package for your website will have both storage limitations (half a dozen high-resolution one-minute videos may well use all of your allowance) and bandwidth restrictions – the more hits your website receives, the greater the bandwidth it requires.

Anyway, these technical limitations are overcome by hosting the videos on YouTube rather than on your own web space.

Safety

YouTube is virus-free, which means that many more corporate systems will allow access to YouTube than might allow the download of videos from random sites, which are not necessarily secure. Also, there is a function for people to report content as inappropriate, so generally the videos themselves are pretty safe for all audiences.

Why is it important?

Well, aside from the technical reasons for wanting to be part of the YouTube universe, there are some rather more human reasons.

Much research has been undertaken about differing learning styles – some people learn best through listening or by watching or by doing. Very few learn best by reading, yet we still insist on filling our websites with words rather than with images and videos (myself included). I'm not saying you should dispense with words altogether, but you should be trying to give people the option of watching a video if they want to. If this is their preferred method of learning (about your business) they're more likely to be able to understand and respond to your messages if you give them a way of learning that they're comfortable with.

> you should be trying to give people the option of watching a video if they want to

It also gives them a chance to get to know you as a person. We all feel that we know Jeremy Paxman better than we know William Shakespeare – this is in part down to the fact that we've only read the works of Shakespeare but we've seen Paxman many times on television. In many businesses the relationship is based on the personality of the people involved and nothing will communicate this better than a video.

Now this is the part that's really important. It's like the video equivalent of the 'be honest' nature of social media in general. You don't want everyone to like you. You don't want everyone to be your customer. What you want is for the people who *really want to be your customers* to be your customers. The proof is in three parts.

1   YouTube has 800 million unique viewers per month. Would you like 800 million telephone calls each month? Probably not, as that's 18,500 per minute all day every day.

2   Do you want to be yourself? Probably yes, because it leads to a more relaxed and fulfilling working environment.

3   Do you want long-term relationships with your customers? Probably yes, then you can spend more time charging for what you do and less time trying to recruit new clients.

Because of this you can be very forthright about who you are and what you want. Many people won't like this, but with such a huge global pool of people it's OK. Probably you want fewer than 100 new customers every year – if you do, you can afford for only 1 in 8 million YouTube visitors to engage with your message.

So, be yourself, be honest and be relaxed … the rest will come.

As I often say to audiences, 99.9 per cent of the people who watch me on YouTube think I'm obnoxious … which is fine because it saves me getting in the car and driving for an hour to have a meeting with someone for them to arrive at the conclusion that they don't like me! It's a great time-saving tool. This is, of course, a bit of a joke, but it illustrates the point that you don't have to please all of the people. In fact, you don't even want to try.

You must, though, be honest.

What should you do?

Well, it all begins with setting up an account. Choose a username that is appropriate (you may need to open a new account if you are already a YouTube user and have a username that isn't appropriate for your business needs).

Once you have created your account, you need to add a bit of personalisation to it. Begin by choosing a layout – perhaps the Blogger layout to start with, listing all video uploads with the most recent (and presumably the most relevant) at the top.

Then choose a background colour (one from your brand colour palette is a good idea) to make sure that the channel is in keeping with the rest of your corporate communications.

The next thing to do is add a background. For this you can use pretty much any image you like that you think reflects what you do and what you're like – the only limitation is it must be smaller than 2MB in file size.

If you're handy with a camera, or a photo-editing package, you might want to create a custom background image. You can see how this looks by visiting my YouTube channel – www.youtube.com/theadamgray. In this instance what I've done is laid out some interesting-looking and fun technology items on the floor in a couple of rows and photographed them.

It would be simple enough for you to do something similar. The more interesting you can make it, the better, as you want to work as hard as possible to capture a visitor's imagination and give them something interesting to look at while they're visiting your page.

There's now the opportunity to add a bit of detail about what you do and how this relates to me, the visitor. A brief summary here is all that's required. The job of this summary is to pique the interest of any visitor and to encourage them to either subscribe to your videos or click through to one of your other places on the internet – perhaps Facebook, LinkedIn or your website – and it is these places where the real conversion work will be done.

So a good idea is to add some links to the profiles that you want people to visit. Your website should certainly be one of them.

> add some links to the profiles that you want people to visit

Shooting your videos

The most common complaint I hear is, 'I can't afford a video shoot'. This is very possibly true as studio time plus a professional videographer can be very expensive … so it's a good job that you don't have to.

The only people who need to have a YouTube channel where every video is professionally produced are … professional video producers. Part of the charm of YouTube as a marketing channel is that there's an honesty and a sort of 'vox pop' quality to it. As long as the video isn't just off the top of your head and as long as it isn't too wobbly, it will be good enough. Most people now have smartphones that have video capabilities (and the opportunity to upload immediately) and in most cases this will be enough. The fact that it's immediate is worth more to the social media world than the fact it's beautifully produced. The things that make a video good in the world of YouTube are 1) is it interesting, 2) is it short and 3) is it honest?

1 *Is it interesting?* Once again we come back to the old chestnut WIIFM (what's in it for me). Does the watcher of your video really want to hear about your latest sales success? *No!* Does the viewer want to hear about your 'brand values'? *No!* Does the viewer want to hear about your products and services? *No!* The viewer wants to learn something. If you are

an expert, the viewer wants you to share some of your expertise and to educate him or her with it.

2 *Is it short enough?* I know that what you're talking about is important to you … that's why you're talking about it, but is it important to me? Probably not as much as it is to you. An amazing fact about the internet world in which we live is that most people who visit YouTube to watch a music video don't watch it right the way through – and that's only three minutes – and it's something they've specifically sought. So they're not going to want to spend ages looking at one of your videos. Generally, in the world of YouTube one minute is a lifetime … 30 seconds is probably a better bet.

3 *Is it honest?* One of the things about video is that it's a very difficult medium to tell lies in. If you aren't being yourself or are not telling the truth about what you know or what you do, the chances are that people will see right through it (and you).

When you're shooting the video it's a good idea to be as relaxed as possible. I have helped a number of clients produce some video blogs and one of the things that really stands out is how difficult it is for many people to talk to camera in a relaxed and natural manner. Even people who are quite comfortable talking to an audience sometimes go to pieces when they have to talk to a camera, so it's probably a good idea to do a bit of practising before sitting in front of the camera for the first time.

> do a bit of practising before sitting in front of the camera for the first time

Don't read a script. Lawrence Olivier couldn't do it so I very much doubt that you can, but that's OK. Just think about the point (or perhaps two points) that you want to make, then talk about it/them for a minute.

It really is as easy as this – you do it with clients every time you meet them, so just think of your video camera as a client. Relax, deep breath and then away you go.

'Hi, I'm Adam Gray and I'd like to tell you why X is such a great opportunity for your business ... and don't forget ... so why not drop me a line if you need any help with this. Good luck.'

It is that simple and, because it's a video, it doesn't matter if you take 50 attempts to get something you're going to be happy with.

brilliant tip

So here are my top five tips for shooting a successful YouTube video.
1   Practise what you're going to say, but don't learn lines (every time it should be different).
2   Do it somewhere comfortable – make the viewer feel at ease. Perhaps sitting at your desk, walking across a field or even sitting in your car.
3   Keep it short.
4   Don't sell – this is not an advert (remember, people make cups of tea during adverts).
5   Keep it short. I know we've already had that one but it really is that important.

Once you've created the account, customised how it looks with a corporate colour, added a background and shot and uploaded a few videos, you're off and running. You have created an outpost in the video world of YouTube and now you have to start to use it.

It's really important you remember that in order for people to be able to find your video clip you must title it, describe it and tag it appropriately. Give it a clear title, so people know what they're looking at – 'Keynote speech at the CIM Digital

Bootcamp' might be an appropriate title – then describe it. 'Adam Gray speaking at the Hertfordshire Digital Bootcamp run by the Chartered Institute of Marketing for Hertfordshire-based SMEs.' Then tag the video 'Social Media', 'Keynote', 'Adam Gray', 'Digital Bootcamp' and anything else that people might be searching for for which this video is the right solution.

It's really important to remember that how you title it should be based on what the person will be searching for, *not* what you necessarily want to call it, so 'My Favourite Talk' or 'Adam does it again!' might be my way of cataloguing the talk ... but it probably won't be yours.

Within your own online ecosystem, sharing flow of traffic from one site to another is a key element of success. Allowing users to move with a single click from your website to YouTube, to Twitter and back to the website is normal and expected behaviour. So it is something that you're going to have to do and get used to. People aren't trapped on one website and they're not trapped on your profile – they can browse all over these networks. The thing that will keep calling them back to you will be controlled by the quality of your content and how much help you give them while they're visiting you.

So putting a link to your YouTube channel on your website and on your LinkedIn profile would perhaps be a good starting point. Make sure that you put plenty of interesting content where people are actually going to be looking for it and make sure that you serve up educational and advisory clips in bite-sized chunks so that people really do leave thinking that the time they spent on your profile was well worth investing.

> make sure that you serve up educational and advisory clips in bite-sized chunks

 **brilliant** recap

- YouTube is the second-largest search engine on the internet (after Google) and gives you the chance to engage your audience in a way other than by writing.

- You must keep the videos short and punchy for best effect.

- While in most cases you don't need to have a professional videographer to film you, you must make sure that the video is clear and not too shaky and you must be natural and relaxed. This is a chance for your prospects to see not only whether you're an expert or not but also if they like you.

CHAPTER 12

The best of the rest: Flickr/ Picassa/ Pinterest

They are three of the most important image-sharing sites. Flickr (part of Yahoo!) and Picassa (part of Google) operate in a broadly similar way.

How do they work?

With each of these sites you can upload your photos to the cloud and store them for future use, so from this perspective every person who takes photos should be using these sites. Often after a house fire people are most upset about losing their photo albums and memories. By using Flickr/Picassa there's an extra level of security for your photos because they are effectively stored in a different location from your physical albums.

Once these photos have been uploaded you can give them different levels of visibility – just you, registered users, friends or everyone.

What are the benefits?

Against each of your photos that you upload you can apply a series of 'tags' or labels to help you identify them. Usually we would tend to title them something personal for ourselves, such as 'Dave's 21st Birthday' or 'Family Christmas 2012', which is great if we are the only ones trying to access them.

If, however, you make your photographs visible to everyone (not the family ones, of course), tag them in a way that people might be searching to find the solution to a specific business problem.

As all of these tags will be indexed by Google and will show up alongside general text-based web pages and YouTube videos in the search results, using photographs (particularly interesting or eye-catching ones) may be a great way of breaking on to the first page of search results.

So, from a solely social perspective, Flickr and Picassa are probably of limited use to most businesses – for photography businesses, of course, yes they're a great resource and probably one that most people should have. Yes they allow interaction, but I guess that for most businesses – even visually based, such as design agencies – their work doesn't translate into a purely pictorial environment. It still requires some explanation and therefore conversations will not appear around images of their work. Clearly if you run an art gallery or are a photographer this possibly isn't true, but generally there are better platforms to invest time in. However, Pinterest is a totally different kind of image-sharing site and one that seems to be creating a real sense of community among users.

Pinterest

What is it?

Pinterest is another image-sharing site, like Flickr and Picassa, but with Pinterest you sign up and then create a series of 'pinboards' of images that interest you. Perhaps things that you think are beautiful, things you've bought, things you want to buy, etc. Then you 'pin' to your various boards images that you have found from around the internet, around Pinterest and you yourself have uploaded.

You follow your friends, they follow you and, through searching for specific things of interest, you can find new people to connect with.

One of the odd things about Pinterest is that it has gone from launch to being quite a compelling and interesting site in a very short space of time. I'm not saying that it will replace Facebook, LinkedIn or any of the other major social hubs in the short term – or indeed ever – but it certainly offers a great respite from the interactions that you'll have on Facebook, Twitter and the like.

In the world of Pinterest people celebrate the beauty of 'things' for their own sake and you can quickly generate quite a large and loyal following just by repinning other people's interesting photos to your own pinboards.

> in the world of Pinterest people celebrate the beauty of 'things' for their own sake

So how do I sign up?

You begin, not surprisingly, by creating an account. You can either do this by using your email address and a password or by logging in using Facebook/Twitter (although there is always an inherent hacking risk of tying all accounts together).

Once you have created an account you have a blank canvas ... or perhaps I mean a blank pinboard! Anyway, by default you have a few blank pinboards created, so probably a good starting point is to rename these to make your account more personalised. You can call them anything you like (you can always rename them if you want to), so perhaps ...

- things I so want to buy
- things I've spent my hard-earned money on
- great places I've found while travelling
- funny things.

Try to make the title of each of the pinboards both fun and indicative of what's actually going to be on it.

As the people who follow you see the new things that you pin to your boards, they can repin them if they choose (this is the Pinterest equivalent of a retweet) and all of their followers will then see the image that you pinned to your board.

If you want to grow your influence on Pinterest the key thing that you'll need to do is to tag your images in an appropriate manner. Of all the concepts that I talk about in this book, one of the most important is 'social proof' – the idea that people's behaviour is more important to your success than being right. Here on Pinterest, it is perhaps truer than most sites. Labelling a great shot of your latest toy in a clever and witty way is all well and good, but remember that everyone will be searching for 'iPad' and nobody will be searching for 'MyPad'. So the fact that MyPad is a nice little play on 'My iPad' isn't the point – the point is it will never be found and, from this perspective, there's little value in uploading the image if it's never going to be discovered.

As with all social media sites you need to remember that the people who are on the site don't necessarily share your passions and interests, so bland photography of a boring product isn't likely to receive loads and loads of followers and comments.

> what Pinterest shots need to be successful is some funky photography

What Pinterest shots need to be successful is some funky photography of some interesting subjects and a series of tags that enable people to find your image.

As I said, for such a simple site that offers so little functionality, there's a fantastic sense of engagement and community. Also unlike some of the other networks, getting started with Pinterest certainly won't be a hardship as it requires pretty much no set-up effort whatsoever and is great fun to use.

 **recap**

- Image-sharing sites offer yet another way that you can engage with your audience.
- Some people prefer written words, some people prefer videos ... and some people are very visually biased.
- From a search perspective you might find that it's easier to get on to the first page of Google results with an image than it is with a page of text, but for maximum effect make sure you name and tag the images properly – 'my_logo.jpg' probably isn't going to help promote your company.

The best of the rest – other social media sites worth a look

All of the sites above are major players in the social space or are rising stars that you might want to be keeping an eye on. The next few sites are a bit more niche. That doesn't mean they're of no use to you and it certainly doesn't mean you should definitely use them, as you probably have a finite amount of time to spend developing your social presence. However, it is worth noting these sites even though they probably won't be on your first tier of platforms unless they particularly offer a benefit to your business.

Instagram

This is a funny one as it qualifies in so many areas. It's an image-sharing social network (where you can have friends and comment on/re-share others' photos). It's an app (for iPhone and android) that lets you take a shot, apply an effect and then share to a variety of other networks (Facebook, Twitter, Flickr, Foursquare, Tumblr – and email). Also, it's now part of Facebook as it was bought it in 2012, so it probably could be called a plug-in too.

It's quite a nice tool as it enables you to create eye-catching photos and develop a style that generally wouldn't be possible to do without the use of Photoshop or a similar image-editing package.

It's certainly worth having a play with this, as it has a strong followership, makes your life easier ... and is great fun!

> it has a strong followership, makes your life easier ... and is great fun!

Foursquare

This is an online game where people check in on the game when they visit places in the real world – 'Adam has checked in at Starbucks in Oxford Street', for example. Foursquare keeps you abreast of what all your friends are doing and also lets you know who has checked in at the venue you are currently visiting. So while I'm at Starbucks on Oxford Street, I might see a further dozen notifications of new visitors, whom I can then introduce myself to if I choose.

If I have the highest number of check-ins to a particular venue, then I am declared 'the Mayor', which is nice!

Now, this might seem like a bit of a flippant use for a social platform for business and indeed it is ... unless your business is a restaurant or bar. If you can incentivise people to check in with their friends by perhaps offering the Mayor a free drink, the fame of your venue can spread far and wide. The cost for this? The drink that you offer today's Mayor.

Foursquare is quite a good resource for its members as it offers a way of cataloguing the feedback and impressions of each venue from your own network. Searching for 'restaurants' close to your location will often give some insight into the atmosphere or experience that otherwise you wouldn't have known until you'd arrived and sat down.

On the downside, Foursquare and a lot of its facilities are now available on both Facebook and Google Places and the advantage that both of these networks have is that they are much larger and therefore have a greater spread.

The idea of crowdsourcing

Over the years much research has been undertaken about 'the wisdom of crowds'. It seems most research concludes that a crowd, pretty much irrespective of their individual intelligence, will be better at performing tasks than an individual ... no matter how clever the individual is.

As in the old days when you went to the fairground and had a go at guessing how many coins there were in a bottle, as an individual you would probably be miles away from the correct answer ... but someone always won!

Prior to the advent of social media the idea of crowdsourcing was very difficult to implement as people were not able to easily mobilise large networks of individuals that were able to discover and curate the necessary volumes of content. Now, there is a plethora of possibilities for you to leverage the knowledge that a disparate group of individuals has (perhaps you have never met them or never will).

All crowdsourcing sites work in a similar way. You join the network and you share valuable content on the site. Other users vote on this content (good or bad) and the aggregated score for each article determines its position.

This sort of site is quite good for delivering unbiased views. Because it is entirely open, and none of the articles goes through a single point of entry, it is difficult to force an outcome. Typically there will be a mix of news, current affairs, informative articles and humour on the site. Because of this it can form an important source of news for its users.

Sites that fall into this category include Digg, Newswire, YahooBuzz, Amplify and, the most popular, Reddit.

Reddit

A simple sign-up procedure, then you're away. You can have a browse around and, on your travels around the internet, if you see any interesting content, you can submit a link to Reddit. Then, depending on how the community feels about the content, it may become popular and start to drive traffic towards that site.

Now, part of the point of social media and social sharing in particular is to share good content to the community without necessarily hoping to get anything back. However, if the content is good, there's obviously no harm in sharing some links to your own site (as well as others) on Reddit – if the content is good enough you may start to see a noticeable increase in traffic to your own site.

Social bookmarking

Typically, companies (and individuals) need to undertake research from time to time. This may be as simple as 'to find a local pizza restaurant', which won't take too long or contain too much risk. However, it might be quite complicated and time-consuming, such as determining 'how many competitors there are in the marketplace and what their specific product offerings are'. Tasks like this are by nature very time-consuming and often need to be undertaken frequently and by several functions within the business. Many of these other departments will go through the same process of searching websites that I have already been through. This leads to a huge duplication of effort. If I have to do the same task twice every year and so do another 9 departments within the business and each review takes 2 days ... that's 40 days per year wasted on duplicating work that's already been done. The simple solution is to store (or bookmark) the sites that deliver the answers and share them across the company.

Now, consider this bookmarking of websites is to be shared beyond just the company and across the whole internet. The more people who bookmark a particular site, the higher it ranks. So, given that crowdsourcing works, it's not unreasonable to assume that the best sites will be those that receive the most votes.

> the more people who bookmark a particular site, the higher it ranks

It is on this basis that sites like Drigo, Mr Wong, Digg and StumbleUpon work.

StumbleUpon

In much the same way as Reddit works, StumbleUpon enables you to sign up and then register the bookmarks for the sites that you think are worth sharing with everyone. The more votes that a site gets, the higher it's rated.

The nature of these sorts of crowdsourced apps means that people are introduced to things perhaps they wouldn't normally see and, most importantly, interesting and fresh content tends to percolate upwards.

If you have content on your site (or someone else's site that talks about you) and it's interesting/valuable, then this kind of crowdsourced marketing can be quite an effective way of spreading the word about your product or service. Irrespective of whether this kind of marketing can work for your business or not, it's a fascinating way to see the world without ever having to leave the comfort of your own sofa!

Content presentation

Because the social world is about sharing information, it means that there's a huge volume of current (and old) content available for you. This means that if you can sort this information you can have the content you actually want delivered to you – as opposed to the content someone else wants. You can see more about this in the 'Tools that are for consuming' section of the book (Chapter 17).

It is worth saying, though, at this stage that much of what I cover here is about you creating – profiles, content, presence – but part of the joy of social media is what you can learn and how you can discover, as well as be discovered.

Eventbrite

Does your business ever run events, perhaps seminars, client briefings or lectures? If so then Eventbrite may be an interesting tool for you to explore. Eventbrite is a ticketing tool that allows you to market, manage and even collect the money for events.

Once you've signed up it's a simple process to create a new event, design the invitations and add logos and maps to make the event look personalised and professional. You can even mail out to your database through Eventbrite and share the event with your friends on Facebook. You can select how many tickets there are, you can set a price for the tickets, you can even create voucher codes to offer incentives to people to book. Then, once you've sent out the invitations, you can monitor in real time how many people have viewed the event and how many have bought a ticket.

Eventbrite automatically charges a commission on all tickets sold and deposits the rest in your nominated bank account.

At the start of 2013 Eventbrite had already sold more than 86 million tickets to events around the world.

As a free platform that offers so much in terms of mailing list management, event information, invitation design, results tracking, transaction and merchant services and tools to help you promote your event, it's no wonder Eventbrite is the largest and best-established of the event management platforms. There's even an iPhone app to help you check people in as they arrive. All of this without the overheads usually associated with professional event management software.

SlideShare

This is a platform to help you share presentations with colleagues and with the world, which I suppose for most businesses at first glance doesn't have a lot of practical benefit. A presentation isn't a book, because it needs a presenter, and without such will be rather lacking in impact.

As with so many social platforms, the sign-up process is fairly straightforward and can be completed in just a couple of minutes, either by choosing a username and password or by signing in with LinkedIn or Facebook. As with most other social platforms, there's a profile page where you can enter a summary about what you and your business do, and there's the opportunity to add a link to your website (good for your SEO) – another touchpoint on the internet for you and your message.

It also offers the opportunity to present your message to a completely new audience. To maximise this opportunity you need to make sure that you tag the presentations with the terms that you want them to be found for. This belt and braces approach will make sure that you are wringing every bit of value from any of the work you do in the social space.

it also offers the opportunity to present your message to a completely new audience

Endomondo

In this modern era of tech-inspired health, Endomondo is among the leaders of the health apps. With Endomondo you can encourage your friends to comment on your fitness achievements as the real-time GPS tracking app keeps your friends updated as to where you're going and how fast you're getting there. Whether you're cycling across the country or just running around the block, Endomondo tracks your progress over time and reports this back to those people you've approved. It works with a wide range of phones and new ones are being added all the time.

Of course, Endomondo is not the only social fitness app. There are literally dozens to choose from – Run Keeper, My Fitness Pal, Map My Fitness, Runtastic, Garmin Fit. It's a very long list. Some of these require you to buy widgets, such as the Nike Fitness Pro (a little chip that attaches to your shoe). Some of them use your phone's inbuilt GPS to track you, but what they all have in common is that they leverage the power of your network to help motivate you and, from your perspective, give you another tool to have conversations and engage with your network.

Clearly, if you are a management accountant there's not a huge amount of synergy between what you do at work and running/cycling at the weekend, but that's kind of the point. You are, I'm assuming, a rounded individual. You do more than just turn up at the office and do a day's work. You have a life. Leveraging these other facets of your personality and using them to create synergy with like-minded people is one of the hidden strengths of social media.

For many years business was conducted in the clubhouse of the golf course because a shared love of golf gave people a platform upon which they could get to know one another and from this friendship flowed business. These days it's not just golf. Cycling is the new golf, so, while at the weekend you are sharing and engaging with your prospects about cycling, you're getting closer to them and edging out your competitors.

Blogging

Blogging could take up a whole book by itself, so this is a very truncated view of what a blog brings to the table from a marketing perspective. Although not strictly social media, blogging is a social media activity (social media being or user-generated content, or, UGC) and is perhaps one of the more important things that you can do to establish you and your business as an expert in your field. A blog (short for weB LOG) is basically just a diary, although, from a business perspective, of course, you would want this diary to focus not on what you've done for the day but on what is of interest to your industry.

Although potentially less about interaction (although you can, of course, get some interaction with blogging) and more about giving you a platform to express your views and thoughts, a blog is beneficial in a couple of ways.

1 The blog is very attractive to Google (and other search engines) because a blog is generally seen by the search engine as one long page (and therefore it contains many keywords), but also because a regularly updated page is much more attractive a destination for the search engine to send visitors to because it's current.

2 It demonstrates that your business is dynamic and has comments to make and opinion on things that are happening as they happen.

However, keeping a blog going is quite a commitment. It requires a constant stream of articles that showcase the talent within the business and this takes time and effort, but in the long run this will undoubtedly pay off. The search engines are likely to deliver more traffic to the site and visitors are likely to be able to find more of interest once they are there.

Blogs should be the heart and soul of any company's website – totally different from the static 'marketing-led' content of the other pages. They should give visitors an opportunity to really get under the skin of the business, identify with the personalities of the various bloggers and feel that they are starting to get to know both the individuals and the company as a whole.

blogs should be the heart and soul of any company's website

Clearly, though, because blog entries are short essays rather than just a few words, the quality of writing required is far higher than with other social media platforms.

brilliant example

Although these may appear to be disparate platforms, many of them can talk to one another: LinkedIn talks to Twitter, Eventbrite talks to Facebook, SlideShare talks to LinkedIn, Endomondo talks to Facebook, Flipboard talks to Facebook, LinkedIn and Twitter ... the list goes on.

This interconnectedness of the various platforms and their ability to share information and content back and forth are part of their strength.

The fact that you have a successful run using Endomondo and all of your Facebook friends can cheer you on or the fact that your new presentation that you've uploaded to SlideShare is immediately shared on LinkedIn means that some of the profile-raising and marketing you have previously had to undertake as a separate task now can happen as a result of you doing the things you would be doing anyway. This interconnectedness of platforms is an exciting by-product of being active in the social media world.

brilliant recap

- Clearly there are strong similarities between the operational characteristics of the various social networks. This shouldn't be a surprise as they all have a great deal in common – us.

- The success or failure of a social network is for the most part driven by how easily we can adopt it as part of our routine. The more closely the network mirrors our in-built behaviours, the more likely we are to take to it easily.

- In essence, all social media networks do the same thing. They enable relationships and conversations between people. With Facebook this may be your close friends, with Twitter it may be celebrities and people you admire, with LinkedIn it may be people you work with (or want to work with) – but whichever network it is, it should connect you, it should move you closer to people and it should enable conversations where there were none.

- The networks you gel with, those that seem to give you the most, will be the ones that either you or your connections feel comfortable with *and* those you can make part and parcel of your everyday life. For this reason, mobile usage is so important ... but more on that in Chapter 17.

PART 3

Making social media work harder

So much to do, so little time …

If you've got this far through the book (assuming that you've done what I've said) you will have a good grasp of how (and why) social media works, you will have created accounts on all the major social platforms, you will have personalised these and you will have populated them with content.

You may already be seeing benefits from reading what people within your network are doing and you might be seeing some opportunities coming in, particularly from LinkedIn.

You probably have also noticed that reading updates from your contacts within all the social platforms and keeping each of these platforms current is quite time-consuming. While you'd like to think that perhaps the people you're connected to are reading what you're posting on each of these platforms, there doesn't seem to be much evidence of it. Perhaps you have a couple of hundred Twitter followers or LinkedIn connections and you have been regularly posting things and there doesn't seem to be much response from your followers (either retweets or comments).

So let's take each of these issues in turn – reducing the time burden, starting to measure the results, increasing the number of responses, growing your influence, getting noticed.

CHAPTER 13

Tools to better manage your social media accounts

One of the issues you might be facing is the sheer number of pages that you need to keep visiting to stay on top of all your social media platforms. Staying on top of all these is particularly important because all these networks are in real time, so people expect swift responses if they make a comment or ask a question.

Typically, if you are active on just Twitter, Facebook and LinkedIn, you might need to visit the pages shown in the table. That's a total of 10 pages and, if you were conscientious, you might want to do this every hour. Consider also that this 10-page investment you're making isn't growing your network, posting updates, researching new clients, it's just responding to what's happening to you. Don't panic, though. Help is at hand.

Twitter	Facebook	LinkedIn	
What's happening	Timeline	Newsfeed	
Connections	Mentions/interactions	Comments	Notifications
Messages	Direct messages	Messages	

There are various tools to pull the content that's important from all of these various places and put it all on the same page for you. New tools are coming out all the time, but three of the easiest and the most popular to have a look at are:

- Sprout Social
- HootSuite
- TweetDeck

What do they do?

They all do basically the same thing – they collect together all the feeds from your various networks and they deliver them to one place so you have far fewer pages to visit. They also allow you to write an update and then, at the click of a button, send it to whichever network(s) is (are) appropriate and respond to incoming messages too. Most of them also have a scheduling function that enables you to write an update and then send it at a later time or date. So if there are various things that you want to say but don't want to say them now because you're worried about bombarding your followers with too many things over a short period, you can write them, schedule them and forget them, knowing that they will be sent later.

As you develop your social presence, using tools can really help to streamline your experience and that of your followers as you can spend more time engaging with people and less time switching back and forth between websites.

The fact that you have so many things in the same place also means you're less likely to miss something important or forget to update your status on certain networks, which is easily done if you have five or six profiles to keep on top of.

using tools can really help to streamline your experience

Sadly, though, there is no tool that works with every single social platform.

Sprout Social is great with Twitter, Facebook and, to a lesser extent, LinkedIn and Google+. You can also (at a cost) add Google Analytics. Sprout Social also offers the best reporting functionality I've seen so far from a tool at this price, delivering oodles of attractive, easy-to-read reports that give real insights into the success you're having.

HootSuite is good, with a larger number of platforms, including Foursquare and WordPress (the blogging platform). It offers some good reporting functions (though not as attractive or easy to read as Sprout) and offers Google Analytics integration at a very low price. However, at the time of writing, there is some confusion as to whether or not HootSuite will fall foul of some restrictions that are shortly going to be placed on how third-party applications can replicate the Twitter stream. Of course, I'm not suggesting you shouldn't use HootSuite as your tool of choice, merely that this is another example of what happens in the fast-paced world of social media and how changes can have a large impact on your day-to-day experience of both the social networks themselves and the tools you choose to access them.

Unlike Sprout and HootSuite, which are web-based tools that you access through your browser, TweetDeck is both browser-based and is an application you can download to your machine. It offers some great Twitter and Facebook functionality (though these are currently the only two supported networks) and is particularly good at saving and displaying search results. For example, you might want to save a search term for 'London Accountant', then you will be notified every time this term is used within a tweet. This can be particularly useful if you are using Twitter to locate some transactional business.

How much do they cost?

Of course, there are many such tools available. Some are free, some are nearly free for a basic package (usually a sub of £10/ month), some more advanced features sometimes increase the cost a little bit, but basically these platforms are a really good idea to make the time spent on social networks work harder for you and for your business. I am always experimenting with new social media management tools because, like social media itself, this is a dynamic industry and things tend to change quickly.

Of course, there is a level of significantly more advanced (and expensive) tools that may run into several hundred or even thousand pounds per month (and are more suited to larger brands with higher levels of traffic). They are able to give detailed analysis on what's being said about your brand in the social space. These tools, such as Radian6 (now part of Salesforce) and Meltwater, require more setting up and a degree of training because of their complexity, but it is fair to say that the insight they offer about what people really think of your brand is nothing short of extraordinary.

When choosing a management tool the two most important criteria are a) does it talk to the social platforms that you want to be on and b) does it deliver the right sort of reports in the right way to you? Reporting (and measurement) is one of the key elements in professionalising your social presence. Whether you are a marketer in a larger business who needs to show your manager that your social channels are engaging more people as time goes by or you are the owner-manager of a business who wants to see that social media is delivering increased web traffic and therefore revenue, the return on investment (ROI) journey starts with understanding what happens when you post an update – how many people read it and how many of them click the link.

We'll look in more detail at attributing ROI in Chapter 16, but by using management tools you have the opportunity to start to put in place a framework to measure your success ... and to grow it too.

CHAPTER 14

How to measure your success in social media

Measuring success in social media is all about understanding how people are behaving rather than how you hope they are behaving. When visitors come to your website you can track them with cookies and Google Analytics (or a similar tool), but when they're on Twitter and you are sending them to another website it isn't so easy. A personalised, shortened URL is the first step in starting to understand their behaviours.

How to track visitors

Whilst on Twitter you may well have noticed a web URL that looks different from usual URLs – this might well be a 'shortened URL'. This was originally developed for use on Twitter (because of the 140-character limitation to tweets) and is where a unique web address (which can be very long indeed) is shortened to something altogether more manageable.

Let me give you an example. I wrote a blog article, 'Partnerships – why business and personal partnerships are the future of business'. The URL for this post is **http://www.GrayUK. com/2012/05/partnerships-why-business-and-personal-partnerships-are-the-future-of-business** – that's 109 characters in itself, so clearly this creates some problems if I want to share it. The use of a URL shortener is vital.

Once again, there's quite a bit of choice here: there's bit.ly, ow.ly, tinyurl.com, goo.gl and many others. However, some of the management tools have their own URL shorteners, which you will need to use if you're using that specific tool.

If you visit any of these sites you can shorten any URL (no matter how long or short) at the click of a button and receive a unique URL that will redirect traffic to the original destination. So our very long URL becomes **http://goo.gl/e0i0b** or **bit.ly/ UPZO77** or even **http://ow.ly/gHzPi**, depending on which URL shortener you choose. This is very handy as the URLs are much more manageable, but, oddly, this isn't the reason for doing it.

One of the problems that marketers face using traditional media is knowing how many people are actually reading their marketing material. Take the advert you place in the daily paper. The fact that there's a circulation of 400,000 people (your followers on Twitter, for argument's sake) doesn't mean that all 400,000 of them have seen and read your advert, does it? Of course not. Some won't have opened the paper, some will have flicked through, some will have read it but not noticed the advert, some will have seen the ad and not read it, some will have read it ... and some will have written down the URL and visited the website when they got home.

It's exactly like this in the social world. Some people will have read your tweet/update, some won't. Some will have clicked a link, some won't. The difference with digital marketing is that you can measure the results of what you're doing so you know in real time whether it's working or not.

some people will have read your tweet/update, some won't

Identifying how many of your connections and followers are actually engaged – how many of these people you can actually mobilise to do what you want – is the first step in calculating the return on your investment and it begins with using short-ened URLs.

Shortened URLs

So, rather than just visiting the site and shortening a URL, open an account on the site and make sure that every URL you shorten is done while you're logged in (or link the shortener account to your chosen management tool) because then the number of clicks against each URL is logged and may be viewed. That way, when you log in to the site again, you will see some fairly comprehensive statistics on how many people

Figure 14.1 bitly URL shortener

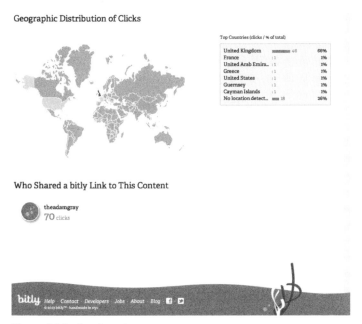

Figure 14.1 Continued

have clicked the link, when they clicked it, how they found the link (Twitter/Facebook, etc.) and where they are, which is very valuable information – see Figure 14.1.

Although this is detailed information about each individual link that you've distributed, if you view this information through the reporting functions of your chosen social media management tool you can see the results in a much broader manner. Figures 14.2, 14.3 and 14.4 are from Sprout Social, but most tools offer similar insights.

This is probably a more valuable way to take an in-depth look at the information. What you're seeing is not the results of an individual URL but the aggregated results of all your activity over the last period – perhaps a day/week/month/quarter – and this is particularly good because it enables you to spot trends.

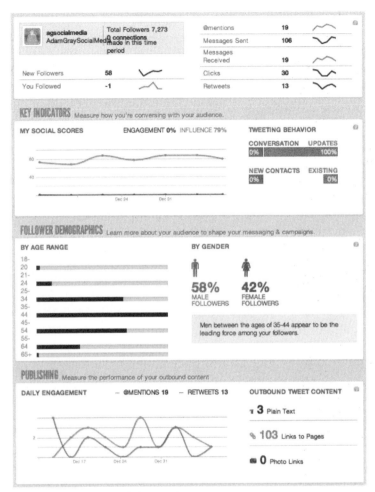

Figure 14.2 Sprout Social general stats

What's important is not to look for the performance of a single comment or post – because you may have written something that just happened to be in the right tone at the right time and has spread virally (this is the digital equivalent of winning the lottery) – but to determine trends among your followers and connections. Because when you can spot a trend or

Figure 14.3 Sprout Social Twitter stats

a behavioural pattern, you can start to tweak the way you do things to deliver more value.

Example

If you're starting to use social media as a business tool – for spreading your message, engaging prospects, talking to existing clients, creating advocates, research and development, for whatever reason – it's reasonable to assume that you want to get as big a response as you can for any given effort. That is because the greater the response, the more efficient what you're doing is.

> the greater the response, the more efficient is what you're doing is

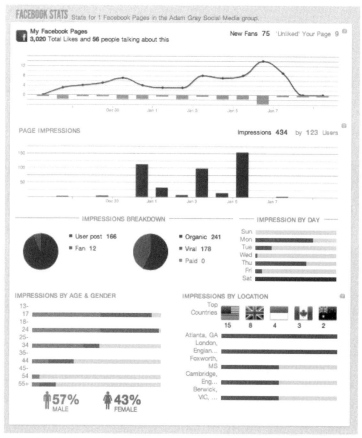

Figure 14.4 Sprout Social Facebook stats

Clearly, some of these will be more successful with your audience than others. If you send a tweet at 10.15 a.m. it may be read 100 times. If you send it at 3.45 p.m., it may be read 160 times. If this pattern repeats each time you try it, you probably would want to send all your future tweets at 3.45 p.m. because they receive 60 per cent more action and more action means more engagement … and more engagement means more benefit.

The same will be true of all the different variables – some will have a big effect, some apparently much less – but if you can establish which give the best results, then this should inform your actions so that you can get the maximum results from any given action.

This refining begins with knowing how people are reacting to your messages. Thinking and knowing are not the same thing and some robust statistics on who's actually clicking the links (the most important measure of how engaged people are) are vital in determining whether you are wasting your time or not.

As you start to measure the number of clicks that you get I would urge you not to be disappointed. As you think about how many people there are on social channels, how many connections and how long they spend reading other people's updates, you cannot expect to get huge percentages of clicks, but that's OK. For every person/company/industry the click-through rate will be different, so don't measure your success by other people's. The important thing is that everything you do is improving your averages.

brilliant tip

There will be many factors that determine how many people read a tweet. These will include:

- when it's sent - a.m./p.m., during lunchtime, during the evening
- how it's phrased - is it a statement, a question, a challenge?
- tone of voice - is it serious, is it funny?
- how many times it's sent - just once or repeatedly.

If you have 1,000 followers and for this month the average clicks per tweet across the 30 tweets that you've sent is 10, then that means you have an average 1 per cent engagement rate. Next month, try tweeting a bit more (not more links, just more tweets) and see if that affects this average. If the average goes up to, say, 12 clicks, then continue with a higher number of tweets. The following month, try changing your tone of voice. Be a little bit more friendly, perhaps tell a joke or two, and see what happens. Perhaps the click rate will drop to 9. If that happens, maybe this isn't working as well, so go back to the previous tone of voice and try something else.

Like so many areas of business, improving things is a process of elimination.

MEASURE – TRY – MEASURE

If you do this repeatedly and see the effects each change has, you can make sure that you're doing more of the right things and fewer of the wrong ones.

An interesting note is that in terms of trying to engage your audience there are no hard-and-fast rules. I get the most response at 1.30 in the afternoon; you probably won't. That's because we have different audiences who do different things, have different interests and respond in different ways. Your audience is different to mine and therefore what you do should be different to what I do.

The trackable URL is a great tool for understanding the behaviours of your followers/connections. The reason it is so valuable and the cornerstone of your measurement strategy is that it is not platform dependent whereas other insights are.

Google Analytics will give valuable and detailed insights about the visitors to your website – time spent, pages visited, where the visitor originated, flow through the site and much more – but it will only deliver this information about your website visitors. So, given that only 25 per cent of your tweets might contain a link to something and only 1 in 10 of those links will

> Google Analytics will give valuable and detailed insights about the visitors to your website

be in your website, this means relying on Google Analytics will deliver insights into the behaviour of your engaged followers for only 2.5 per cent of their time.

Facebook offers some fantastic insights, a bit like Google Analytics but on your Facebook page. It gives information on the size of your universe (fans and fans of fans), how many people are talking about your page (and how this performs against the last period, e.g. +53 per cent), what your 'total weekly reach' is (and how this performs against last week). You can also see over time how your number of 'likes' is increasing, how your reach varies from week to week (through organic, viral and paid methods) and how many people are talking about you.

 brilliant definition

Total weekly reach
This is the actual (rather than average) number of people who have been exposed to your page. It is the sum of the people who have liked and/or commented on your page and all their friends (because if I comment on your Facebook page, all my friends see that I have interacted with you).

YouTube has its own analytics package as well. With this you can see stats on how many videos have been watched, the total user time spent watching them, where the viewers have come from (both by referrer and geographically) and when they came. You can even see how long each of your videos has retained each of the viewers (letting you know if your videos are too long or if there's a particular moment that people don't like).

you can even see how long each of your videos has retained each of the viewers

All of these are valuable for finessing your presence on each of the networks and may be worth focusing some effort on once you are able to determine if any of them are working particularly well for you. Certainly to begin with, the broad strokes reporting provided by one of the management tools will be more than adequate to help you improve your social presence and should be a vital part of your routine.

brilliant recap

Although you might not need the data (or even know what to do with it) to begin with, you should collect it immediately. 'Knowledge is power' – having historic information on how your network behaves and how it reacts to you will be very useful in the future as you start to refine and improve your presence in the social space.

CHAPTER 15

Refining your presence

As with all forms of communication, the biggest thing working against you developing a strong profile is everybody else doing the same thing. On social networks it's no different. The thing that is likely to limit your ability to develop a strong presence is that everyone else is trying to develop a strong profile on these networks.

If you just think about the numbers of updates from everyone in your network you can't read as it is. If you have 200 connections on each of the big four networks and each update takes you an average of a minute to read, that would be (assuming a 50 per cent overlap of content) 400 minutes of status update reading every day ... that's 6¾ hours every day, just reading what other people are doing. That leaves no time for actually doing your work, let alone contributing your own status updates.

The problem is that everyone in your networks is in the same situation regarding viewing everyone's updates, including yours. Unless, of course, you can make yourself stand out from the crowd.

This is not as difficult as it might seem. Despite the huge amount of content that will drift past you during the course of the day, humans are very good at sifting through large volumes of information. Whether you're searching through the

TV listings, the phone book or Twitter, the things that you're looking for, or the people you're looking for, invariably jump out at you.

That thing (or person) that jumps out *must* be you. The question is, how does one achieve this, with everyone else shouting and broadcasting what they're doing?

Remember earlier in the book I said that the world of social media can be very well imagined as a garden party? Well, if you picture your involvement on Twitter, a LinkedIn Group or Google+ as if it were a real-life party, would you:

- expect to turn up and address everyone at the party (and have them listen to you) – *NO*
- expect them all to stop their conversations and listen to you even though they don't know you – *NO*
- expect them to want to discuss the benefits of flambé rather than dry-frying (or whatever your passion is) – *NO*

Then why would you expect this to happen in the online world? Well, of course, you can't. Building a loyal, large, engaged following of people who listen to what you say takes time and effort and is achieved one follower at a time – but it *is* built. You need to develop an authentic voice for you/the business and post engaging content, but first you need to get spotted and that happens best in the same way as it does in real life.

You know from your experience at the garden party that the guy who just wants to talk about himself is the most boring person there. You know that he's not interested in you because he's too busy talking about himself. You know that you can't wait to get away and if you see him walking up to you later in the party you need to find someone else to talk to, anybody, and fast! But the person who listens intently when you talk, who asks intelligent questions to clarify points about you and waits to be asked before talking about him- or herself is a joy to spend time with.

You need to find your own 'online' version of being Mr or Ms Interested. It might be as simple as responding to a good article that someone has shared like this: 'Thanks for finding a fantastic article, you also might want to read this similar one' might be a good starting point or even a, 'Brilliant, thanks for sharing'. Whatever you do, you need to elevate yourself from being one of

> every tweet and update needs to demonstrate that you are worthy of reading

the masses to being someone who is noticed. Then, once you've been noticed, you need to reinforce that you are someone who adds value. Every tweet and update needs to demonstrate that you are worthy of reading, but you can do this only once someone is reading what you write and the best way to start the ball rolling is flattery!

Imagine it from their perspective. If someone follows you, then says 'thanks, I really enjoyed that', then re-shares what you wrote, then sends a message saying, 'have a look at this research, in a similar vein', it's only a matter of time before you start to pay attention. Once you do, you can't help but notice that person's updates when they crop up in your feed and then there's a chance you'll read them.

There is an old networking adage: 'You have one mouth and two ears, use them in those proportions', and nowhere is this more important than in the world of social media. People can connect with you across multiple platforms at the click of a button, but they can also disconnect if you abuse that relationship by spamming and overloading their streams with your opinions.

You do need to be mindful, however, that social networks are not successful places for people and brands which are overly formulaic in their approach. Yes, you need to do the hygienic stuff like thinking about what people want to read and might be interested in or listening and answering rather than just shouting, but it's more than that. Success comes from finding your own voice, being yourself, being engaging and authentic about who you are and what matters to you.

Who would have thought that Psy, a slightly overweight singer from Korea who looks like he's still living in the 1980s, would have released a video on YouTube and received a staggering 1,400,000,000 views – that's over half a billion views more than global teen heartthrob Justin Bieber's most popular video. Psy achieved this through being himself and it is that authenticity which works in social media (and in life).

Research and development (R&D)

Well, research first. Part of refining your presence is going to involve researching what your contacts, customers and prospects want or need. There are some major problems with conducting research, the first of which is that asking questions can distort people's opinions. For example, if I were to come to your lovely old-fashioned office and you were to ask me which bit I liked the least, I might look around, consider and then say, 'I don't really like that kind of desk.' Now, that's not the same thing at all as me walking into your office and saying, 'Oh, I don't like your desk.'

The fact that you have asked me for an opinion means I have looked for an opinion to give you. The question could have been, 'Are you happy with the service?', '... the charges?', '... your account manager?', 'Do we run enough of the trains on time?'. For each question you would have placed a degree of doubt in my mind and encouraged me to find something to say.

So, a huge amount of effort is often invested in making sure that the questions you ask 'lead' respondents as little as possible. Nevertheless, it is inevitable that it will happen to a certain extent.

The other problem with asking questions is that they can set an expectation of change. Assume if you will that you are a customer of mine and I send you a questionnaire asking you what you would change about the past project if you could change anything and you say, 'The cost – we feel that you charge too much for the services that you provide.' The problem is that once you've told me this, you – rightly – think that I have listened to the response and this will inform my future actions (otherwise why would I have asked the question in the first place?), but I have no intention of lowering my prices ... in fact, I think I should be putting them up. This understandably could cause friction in our relationship – at the very least you're likely to be a bit disappointed that you wanted me to lower my prices and in fact I raised them!

Social media offers you the opportunity to listen to what people are saying (and here's the important bit) without asking the questions first. That means you don't distort results or even let people know you're thinking about a specific area. You just overhear conversations. People use social channels to complain, to ask for advice, to share their experiences – the fact is that people love to talk and with social media monitoring you can really tune in and listen to what they're saying.

The same is true for new product development. You're listening rather than leading. It's like having a global focus group talking about everything from your product to religion, from politics to cookery. All you need to do is to have the right tools to tune in ... and the budget to be able to pay for them.

CHAPTER 16

Social media monitoring

Social media monitoring offers a great business opportunity and should really be part and parcel of every business' processes if they are using social media in any way. Clearly businesses should also have some marketing measurement in place, but with social media you're actually listening to what's being said and what the undercurrent means, it's so easy and the reporting is so clear that there's really no excuse not to.

Social media monitoring should enable you to quickly see the results of your efforts and, if they are unsatisfactory, to identify why they are and improve them. You will do this in real time so problems become opportunities and opportunities aren't missed. So, although this is a big and rapidly changing marketplace, perhaps a good place to start is an overview of some of the more popular platforms along with an indication of a typical cost for using them.

> social media monitoring should enable you to quickly see the results of your efforts

Like so much in life, you get what you pay for. Free tools are a good starting place, as might be the range of low-cost tools, but they are limited in terms of both what they look at and how they report findings, so if you're looking for a free or cheap solution you must be prepared to pull together the results yourself and then present them in a format that makes sense. Some of these tools I have already mentioned.

For ease of use I have split this section into three main areas:

- free monitoring tools and resources
- nearly free tools and resources
- paid-for resources.

Free

- *Google Alerts* are simple to set up and provide emailed warnings every time your key phrase(s) are found by Google as it searches web pages. As a matter of common sense you should have alerts running for your own brand name and for that of your competitors, but you can also use this to ferret-out tactical opportunities and industry changes.

- *Twitter Advanced Search* enables you to perform simple Boolean search strings (and/or/not, etc.). Recently it has started to add sentiment measurement, which is good in theory, but in practice it is difficult to produce accurate results as machines seldom 'get' irony or sarcasm. However, it's still worth doing for specific project work. The addition of a tool such as Seesmic, TweetDeck or HootSuite will enable you to save keyword searches, which can be very handy as an alert to mentions about your competitors or particular projects and trending topics.

- *Icerocket* helps you keep watch over Twitter, blogs, the web, news, images and more. Features include a topic cloud and basic listing of mentions. This social media monitoring tool also offers the ability to bookmark your search results for later reference.

- *Addict-o-matic* is a consolidated page with search matches across a number of different platforms, including blogs, Twitter, Digg and Flickr. It has quite a nice simple interface and one-page dashboard and is a good freebie for summarising all your 'buzz' in one place.

- *BoardTracker* focuses on grabbing 'buzz' from message boards and forums, so if you have a technical, specialist or slightly 'geeky' product, this could be the tool you should have a play with.

Nearly free

- *TwentyFeet* (around $25/year) aggregates all of your Twitter, Facebook, YouTube, bit.ly, Myspace and Google Analytics metrics into one place (more to follow too) and allows you to see everything in one snapshot. It also allows you to get all the tracking benefits of HootSuite without being tied into both its interface and the ow.ly URL shortener. TwentyFeet seems to be taking the low-cost monitoring world by storm, with advocates such as Chris Brogan, Brian Solis and Erik Qualman, the three pioneers of social media analysis, comment and theory.

- *HootSuite* I have mentioned already as a good way to manage your social media accounts, but it's also an exceptional tool for managing multiple accounts and graphing results for engagement and reach and at a mere $5.99/month it's as good as free. It enables you to save searches and catalogue results. The really good bit though is that not only can you track click-throughs from each of your accounts (to get a measure of engagement), but you can also map these results against your Google Analytics to see how social media is driving traffic to your website. A brilliant tool no doubt, just a shame that the interface can't offer aggregated mentions across all platforms in the way that TweetDeck does.

- *Social Report* costs $9/month – well, that is to say you can dip your toe in the water for $9/month. If you want more detailed analytics, ROI tracking and reporting and some CRM capabilities it'll cost $39/month.

- *Trackur* ($18/month) is a comprehensive and easy-to-use package offering similar features to the other 'nearly free' tools available. If you are new(ish) to social media and need to report to the Board about progress, this could be the tool for you as the reports are intuitive and easy to decipher. There are various levels of functionality, but most businesses will probably end up spending either $88/month or $197/month … those looking to brand the reports for shareholder docs … and vanity will need to pay more, though, as visual branding and customisation involves an additional chargeable function.

- *Sprout Social* ($39/month) is not only an analytics aggregator but has a dashboard to interact as well. Monitoring, analytics, research, management and CRM can all be found in one package, plus an android/iPhone mobile app. Very attractive and simple-to-read reports, but if you want access to all the features it will cost you $59/month, although, depending on the number of licences, this could be up to $899 per month for some users.

Paid for

It has been difficult to identify an 'average' cost of these platforms because there are not generally published prices for them. I shall keep up to date with latest trends in both what platforms and tools are available and what the 'average' cost of such platforms is, so if you would like to start using these tools or have any more to suggest then head to **www.GrayUK.com/ brilliant** where you will be able to see up-to-date listings.

This is far from an exhaustive list, but I have noted the most popular, the best regarded and the ones I have some experience of.

- *Brandwatch* ($300/month) trawls the internet looking at news, blogs, forums, wikis and social networking sites and finding mentions of brands, companies, products and people. Clients define keywords (brands, topics, people's names, products) and receive reports and brand summaries that they can take action on.

- **Cost:** Pricing, based on a monthly subscription, starts at about $300/month. It operates on a per keyword pricing model.
- **Clients:** Aviva, Activision, Cheapflights, The Body Shop.
- **Owner:** Independent.

- *Lithium* ($249/month) monitors your search-specific mentions and sentiment in social media outlets and outputs them into easy-to-read graphs and numbers resembling the stock market. Lithium will aggregate information from a variety of platforms, including blog posts and comments, Twitter, Facebook, Flickr and many others, plus it will assess emotions surrounding your brand pre, mid and post campaign so you can adjust your strategies accordingly.

  - **Cost:** $249/month for five users and five searches. Free 14-day trial.
  - **Clients:** Best Buy, BT, Barnes & Noble, FICO, Disney Online, StubHub, Motorola, Coca-Cola, Focus Features, Netflix.
  - **Owner:** Independent. Lithium bought Scout Labs in May 2010.

- *Collective Intellect* ($300+/month), after originally providing monitoring to financial firms, has become a major force in social media monitoring. Using a combination of self-serve client dashboards and human analysis, Collective Intellect offers a robust monitoring and measurement tool suited to mid-size to large companies with its Social CRM Insights platform. It applies spam-management techniques and text analysis to clean data sets, delivering customer rich intelligence.

  - **Cost:** Pricing starts at $300/month and scales based on specific client needs, according to published reports.

- **Clients:** General Mills, NBC Universal, Pepsi, Walmart, Unilever, Advertising Age, CBS, Dole, MTV Networks, MillerCoors, Paramount, Verizon Wireless, Viacom, Hasbro, Siemens.
- **Owner:** Independent.
- *Radian6* ($600/month) is one of the most established and successful monitoring platforms and helps you to listen more intelligently to consumers, competitors and influencers, offering detailed, real-time insights. Beyond its monitoring dashboard, which tracks mentions on more than 100 million social media sites and blogs, it offers an engagement console that allows you to coordinate your internal responses to external activity by immediately updating your blog and Twitter and Facebook accounts all in one spot. Fully automated.

  - **Cost:** The dashboard starts at $600/month. Radian6 uses a monthly subscription-based pricing model, with the fee varying depending on the number of topics monitored each month.
  - **Clients:** Red Cross, Adobe, AAA, Cirque du Soleil, H&R Block, March of Dimes, Microsoft, Pepsi, Southwest Airlines, a wide range of clients.
  - **Owner:** Salesforce.

- *Meltwater* ($13,000) monitors, tracks and analyses user-generated content on more than 200 million social media sites and blogs to help a brand understand its user sentiment and gauge competition. All data is stored in an easy-to-use dashboard and customer support is provided for the duration of the subscription. Meltwater has 50 offices around the globe. It's worth mentioning that they come from a traditional media-tracking background and, with the purchase of BuzzGain in February 2010, it added many more social media monitoring capabilities. BuzzGain is now built in to Meltwater Buzz.

- **Cost:** Standard subscription of one year for $13,000 provides access for three to five users.

- **Clients:** Porsche Automotive North America, Vitamix, St Jude Children's Research Hospital, Bausch & Lomb, Pabst Blue Ribbon and other corporations, non-profits, government agencies.

- **Owner:** Meltwater Group.

- *Twelvefold* (formerly Buzzlogic) uses its technology platform to identify and organise the conversation universe, combining both conversation topic and audience to help brands reach audiences passionate about everything from the latest tech craze and cloud computing to parenthood and politics. However, the social media monitoring tool is no longer available as a standalone product. It now comes as part of BuzzLogic's ad platform, requiring a media buy to connect to unique audiences through BuzzLogic.

- **Cost:** Unknown.

- **Clients:** Starbucks, American Express, HBO, HP, Microsoft. Focus on advertisers.

- **Owner:** Independent.

There's a fair amount of choice at all price points and paid-for resources are big business, helping to underline the importance of measurement as part of a marketing strategy.

The truth is that, even if your business isn't particularly active in the social space (and it should be), you should be listening to what's being said about your brand as a matter of due diligence. Just because you are not represented in the space doesn't mean that people won't be talking about you and your brand ... and as we all know, unhappy customers have very loud voices!

For most companies that have a marketing budget, the investment of a few hundred pounds each year in some kind of listening, cataloguing and presentation platform would be money well spent. For those that are engaging in social media already, to not do so is madness.

⟨brilliant⟩ tip

So, with so many products, which should you use?

At the free end of the scale	A little money	Big money
● Google Alerts	● TwentyFeet	● Meltwater
● Tweetdeck	● Trackur	● Radian6
● Twitter search	● Sprout Social	

For the ones that are free I recommend you try them out and see how you like them. You might feel it is worth spending a little money to get more functionality. Though I wouldn't needlessly advocate spending money, if you can afford it, Radian6 could well be worth it – the results have been staggeringly accurate and insightful and the combination of automated information gathering and human analysis for the reporting means that you really get the best of both worlds.

Let's take a quick look at what using these tools will bring you.

With a tool such as TweetDeck you can put in place some standing searches on Twitter. This means that every time someone uses a key word or phrase you will be notified about this. Clearly, on Twitter you are already notified of comments about your username as a matter of course. So, I get a light on my Twitter homepage when someone references '@theadamgray'; I don't get a notification if someone says 'Adam Gray' or 'Adamgray' or even '#adamgray'. However, to any followers of the person

> every time someone uses a key word or phrase you will be notified about this

who's referenced me or anyone searching for one of these terms then the tweet will be visible, and it's really just fair that I should know about this too.

If you have a Google account (and, I have said this a few times already, if you haven't got one, you should get one) you can set up Google Alerts. These ensure that, as Google trawls around the internet indexing all the web pages, every time the search phrase you've requested is found, you'll get an email telling you. So, every time that a LinkedIn update or a blog post or a website mentions 'Adam Gray', I get an email from Google telling me so. This is very handy as it means that you'll never hear news, good or bad, about yourself from someone else first. Basically this is due diligence: if you or your brand is mentioned, you need to know about it. This can be a little problematic to begin with as you will need to refine the search unless you are in the fortunate position of a friend of mine, Caspar Berry, where there are only two of them in the whole world (the other being a six-year-old boy). Running Google Alerts on your name will demonstrate how many times someone with the same name as you is mentioned on the internet. For me there's a chef, a hairdresser, a rodeo rider and an adult movie actor, all of whom have an internet presence and all of whom share my name. You will probably find something similar and you will therefore need to refine the search to make sure that you only get results for your name when it is tied to something related to what you do.

So, adding these two things – setting up Google Alerts and TweetDeck searches – is the first step on the social media monitoring ladder.

As you move up through the levels of social media monitoring you will see the tools delivering greater and greater customer insight. For example, a restaurant chain might find that typically some people tweet about the awful fast-food restaurant meal they experienced, some might say what good fun they had in the same restaurant, some might say how it represented good value, some might say that the food was too greasy. All of this can be stored so that at a later date the restaurant chain can look at all of these comments.

- Anecdotal comments: 'my meal was cold', 'Dave the manager was rude', 'the table wobbled'.
- Quantitive analysis: 200 people said the food was greasy, 31 per cent said the experience was fun.
- Trend analysis: an increasing number of people said the food was good value (because despite rising costs we've not increased our prices), a decreasing number of people said the food was greasy (because we've changed the recipe).
- Insight into changing desires and behaviours: I wish I could buy a cappuccino in Jojo's restaurant.
- Sentiment analysis: half of the visitors are happy with the experience.

This is a fantastic technique to gain insight into what your customers want and what they really think – better than traditional research because it's covert and therefore your presence isn't distorting the results and it's in real time: you can see the comments as they're happening and if you're agile enough you can respond and change things immediately.

> if you're agile enough you can respond and change things immediately

It also enables you to take the comments like, 'I wish I could buy a cappuccino at Jojo's restaurant' and use this insight to steer new product development and which new lines to stock. More exciting from a business development perspective is the way that social media monitoring allows access to Net Promoter Score information for businesses. This is the ratio of people who are positive about the brand against those who are negative (ignoring those who are neither one thing nor the other, known as passives). This Net Promoter Score is one of the most powerful tools available for determining whether or not a business is on the right track (from a brand perspective) as it is simply a measure of people's feelings towards a brand.

Oddly, if everybody dislikes a company this doesn't mean that it's going to fail or have a rough time, but a change in the Net Promoter Score usually is a precursor to a change in the company's fortunes ... for better or worse.

As we saw in Chapter 14, it's important to know for sure if what you're doing is striking a chord with your followers and whether or not you are moving in the right direction, but this is not the important question from a business perspective. Too often marketing is seen as a cost rather than an investment, too often we don't measure if our advertising campaign has covered its costs or made a profit. In this day and age, when every cost needs to be proven and justified, it simply isn't acceptable to just 'hope' that a campaign has worked or to say 'it's brand building and you can't measure the monetary benefit' because you can ... and you should.

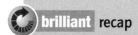 **brilliant** recap

- Measuring how people behave is vital in becoming a sophisticated social media user.

- 'Hoping' that people are reading and engaging with what you say isn't good enough.

- 'Knowing' whether they do (or don't) engage with you is what's required and understanding what you can do better is the way to move from having some success with social media to having it drive your business to new heights.

The process of measuring the return on investment (ROI) on your social media campaigns begins outside of the social sphere and the process looks like this.

How do I measure success?

Warning: this next section contains a couple of simple equations.

For a business, its website is its 'base camp' on the internet. It is the largest online resource and it is the place that is most likely to catalyse action and a sale. A host of web-based tools is available to help you understand what visitors do while they are on your site, but assuming that you use a free one, such as Google Analytics, you can begin to build a valuable picture of what people do on your site. You should be tracking the number of email and telephone enquiries that come from the website. You should also have some idea of the number of new business pitches or proposals you have delivered over the last period.

Given that you have this information (and the clue here for every business is that you *should* know all of this), then you know how many unique visitors to your website it takes to get a) a phone call/email and b) a new customer. If you know what the average lifetime value of a customer is (and you should) then you will be able to calculate how many visitors to the website are required to generate a given amount of money.

So, if it takes 1,000 unique visitors to get a phone call and it takes 25 phone calls to get a customer, it therefore takes 25,000 unique visitors to get a customer. If the lifetime customer value is (for ease of visualisation) £25,000, then each unique visitor is worth £1.

Try this as a start. Put your own figures into the equation in Figure 16.1. This shows you the average value of each website visitor – let's call this average web visitor value (AWVV).

Clearly there are some anomalies in here: a) you may have to get 10,000 visitors before you find the one who buys, b) this is lifetime value of customer and this might be taken over a year, a decade or perhaps even longer. If this is a problem for you, clearly dividing the visitor value by the customer lifetime will give you an annual website visitor value.

A = unique visitors required to get one phone/email lead
B = phone/email leads required to get one customer
C = average lifetime customer value

$$\text{Value of each website visitor} = \frac{C}{A \times B}$$

Figure 16.1 Average website visitor value

Now, it is true of course that this may throw up certain other problems – you're not very good at pitching, perhaps, or the website doesn't work very well – but assuming that things aren't too badly broken you at least have something to work with: knowing this information is important not just for social media but also in terms of understanding the cost and return for all of your online marketing ... and beyond.

Like the measurement scenario, the probable outcome of this isn't very cheery to start with but it is – and this is the most important bit – a stake in the ground against which you can start to measure your improvements.

Once you know the information about how your website converts traffic to money, you apply what you already know about your engagement rate, number of tweets and ratio of tweets that point to your site (as opposed to elsewhere) and hourly cost of staff for maintaining your social presence and there you have it.

Number of followers = say 1,000 for the moment

Remember, engagement rate = clicks/followers (let's say 5%)

Social media cost per tweet = cost per hour (say £25)/tweets per hour (say 10 tweets/hour) = £2.50/tweet (clearly you're not sending ten tweets per hour, but each tweet is taking six minutes)

Ratio = the ratio between tweets and tweets to your site (typically 8:1 or 12.5%)

Using these figures, as in Figure 16.2, the cost per visitor is £2.50 divided by (1,000 followers × 5% × 12.5%) which is 40p.

F = number of followers
E = engagement rate
R = ratio
P = cost per tweet

$$\frac{P}{F \times E \times R} = \text{cost per visitor}$$

Figure 16.2 Social media cost per visitor

So, with this example, using the first equation's results for the average customer value, every 40p you spend running this social media department will return £1 in sales revenue. This may be good/bad/indifferent depending on your business model, but, as I've said before, it's a starting point. Keeping those figures the same but increasing your number of followers to 2,500 means that your cost per visitor is 16p, which is a ROI of 6.25:1 – every £100 you spend delivers £625 of business.

Increasing the quality of your tweets to raise engagement from 5% to 6% and increasing follower numbers to 8,500 means that you get a ROI of 25.5:1, which means that for every £1000 you invest in social media you achieve sales of £25,500.

Note: I have used Twitter as an example here (tweets and followers), but the same equation holds true for Facebook, YouTube, LinkedIn, etc., so, because you're likely to have wildly different engagement rates and network sizes on each of the networks, you will probably need to calculate your ROI from each of these networks individually (but by creating an Excel spreadsheet for all of them together and then just adding in the latest figures, you'll make it relatively quick and easy to do).

It is worth remembering at this point that this may be achievable from the outset or it may require a significant amount of time and effort to refine it to this point. It is also worth saying that this does not take into account any other side benefits, such as increased brand awareness or general good feeling about the company.

Of course, it may be that you don't know the average lifetime customer value or how many visitors you need to get to your website to get a customer, so you should start to put in place some sort of framework whereby you can measure these things, because without them you can't know whether any of your marketing is paying its way, let alone your social media. Even if you don't know the customer acquisition costs, though, you can still benefit from going through this process. What you won't get is a ROI or even any hard figures, but what you will get is a comparison week on week, month on month of whether you are doing things with a greater or lesser success rate and that is how you hone a social media campaign: try, measure, adjust, measure.

Assuming that you do have the numbers to put some solid costs against acquisition, this shows your digital ROI through your non-social channels. Anything that you convert through your entirely social channels or via an online shop is of course far easier than this because you just remove the appropriate bits (there's more on how to personalise this measurement equation available at my website: **www.GrayUK.com/brilliant**). The principle is very straightforward (even if the execution can be a bit fiddly) and the exciting thing about this is that not only can you see how much your social efforts are delivering for your business but also, more importantly, if you think about the fact that the equation is a balance, it enables you to determine exactly what you need to do in order to be able to generate a given amount of sales … so think about that for a moment.

If you know what you need to do to be able to generate a given revenue stream, you can slow it down when you go on holiday or have a large order to fulfil and increase it if it looks like you're heading into a quiet period. How cool is that? You have just created a sales tap that you can turn on and off at will.

you have just created a sales tap that you can turn on and off at will

The reality is it's a little bit more complicated than that because there will be variables, the element of chance, various unforeseen things and the fact there may be a long lead time or delay between performing an action and getting the result, but in principle this is the marketing nirvana we've all been waiting for.

The important point about measurement of ROI is that it raises your awareness about the efforts you make and the cost benefits they deliver and this as often as not increases efficiency itself.

 **brilliant** recap

If you put in place some sort of social media monitoring you will be able to identity within the social media space:

- what your competitors are doing
- what people are saying about you and your brand
- if you are doing a good job
    - whether you are improving your presence or if it's getting worse
    - business opportunities that are appearing in the social media space
    - if your competitors are starting to woo your clients
    - the financial benefit of your social media efforts.

CHAPTER 17

Other things you need to know

This next section covers a few interesting, useful things that you should be aware of but don't really fit into any of the other sections. Because this book is about social media they don't need a full chapter...but you should know them anyway.

Signing in using other social platforms

As you will have seen from signing up for several social platforms, many of them give you the choice of an account or to sign in using (usually) Twitter or Facebook. Clearly there's a bit of an incentive for you to do the latter – just a single click, no passwords to remember as opposed to going through the usual sign-up process.

Often this sign-up process gives the new app or site a series of rights, such as writing on your wall, posting on your behalf or accessing your friends' details. Usually this wouldn't cause a problem. Most of the new sites are trying to integrate themselves as closely as possible with their bigger brother, as Instagram (a photo-sharing application) did with Facebook.

However, you are placing a load of trust in the new app not taking advantage of your Facebook or Twitter account and this could be unwise. Having an account hacked or exploited (by either a person or another site) can be a worrying experience. If you've developed a loyal and engaged following, this will have taken you a lot of time and effort and giving access to these people to someone without your level of commitment is perhaps a little foolhardy – a poorly thought-through comment or something inappropriate being posted in error can cause a lot of damage to those relationships.

We have talked about basic security, but for the time being consider if sharing all your security usernames and passwords across all your social networks is a good idea and whether or not the ease of having just a couple of things to remember outweighs the risk of having all your networks compromised by losing just one password.

Which brings me nicely to the matter of passwords. For some time it has been recognised that passwords, in all their guises, are not secure. Yes, make them longer and they're more difficult to crack, but they are inherently crackable. Multi-stage security (which banks tend to use), where you need a username, a password and a further key, is better, and where multi-level security is an option this should be enabled on all your networks.

Perhaps the biggest issue is *not* sharing passwords across each of your social networks because if you do you could be in all sorts of trouble. Imagine if one of your networks is compromised and you share passwords. This means that the hacker has access to your entire social presence. They can broadcast untrue or unpleasant things across all the platforms on which you've worked so hard to build trust and rapport and that could put your credibility back years.

the hacker has access to your entire social presence

Perhaps even worse, sharing passwords means that your email is vulnerable and this means the hacker can reset all your username and password combinations so you can't get back in, access sensitive emails and find other information, which might be highly confidential, and possibly gain access to your bank account through searching old emails and requesting a password reset. All because you didn't want to have to go through a two-step sign-in process.

Think about that for a moment.

Mobile use

Many of the social platforms have custom-made apps to enable you to use them in a comfortable and natural way while you're out and about. This is really important for you as both a contributor and a consumer of content.

As a consumer of content from the social networks you need to sit and read (either in detail or just a cursory glance) but you need to invest a little bit of time. While sitting at your desk you have a whole host of tasks vying for your attention – client emails, telephone calls, complaints (I hope not), problems, bookkeeping, administration, reporting, colleagues … whatever it is, it seems there's always something for you to do that's either more pressing or more important.

This is a *really* bad thing, because what you should be doing is seeing what others are saying and responding to it, learning and generally listening to news and views. However, with the advent of mobile access, those previous chunks of unproductive time can be turned into something really useful. Waiting for a bus, travelling on a train, stuck in a traffic jam, eating your lunch, lying in bed unable to sleep … whatever the situation, this is a previously wasted opportunity that you can now take if you want to.

There's been a lot of news about 'Facebook fatigue' and people getting 'Twittered out', but as with any other aspect of life you need to handle these things in moderation. I'm not suggesting that you should be on Facebook 24/7; however, with the advent of mobile access you can be if you want/need to be.

This is great for you not just because you can spend more of your time doing the things you should be doing but also so that you can have access to others when they have, in essence, little else to do other than engage with your message. The reason that this two-way street is so crucial is because usually you would try to engage prospects and clients with your message when they have loads of more important things to do (like you) – answering emails, talking to clients, doing admin – but they too, will be using their mobile devices to connect with their networks, to listen as well as talk and to engage with interesting people ... like you!

Usually these mobile apps (available for iPad, iPhone, android, Blackberry and more) give a speedy, device-sympathetic experience for each of the important platforms and at the time of writing almost all the major platforms produce apps for most mobile devices and all of these are free.

Tools that are for consuming rather than creating and sharing

Although Reddit, Technorati, StumbleUpon and the like are tools for sharing good sites, your presence there (and the comments that you make) help to further refine what's hot and what's not. There is another series of tools though (usually apps) designed to deliver the content from your social networks to you and the most popular of these is Flipboard.

Flipboard is a free smartphone and tablet app that takes feeds from your Facebook, Twitter, Google+ and LinkedIn profiles along with more generic newsfeeds (about the topics that you want) and delivers them in an interactive newspaper format to your phone or tablet. Using apps like this really has to be experienced to be believed. Unlike most newspapers, where 80 per cent of the content remains unread because it is

using apps like this really has to be experienced to be believed

not relevant or interesting to you, on Flipboard every single article is either of interest (because it concerns people you know) or relevant (because it's about a topic or industry that you have selected).

This app was recommended to me by a friend and I became an immediate convert. It has helped me to consume more news and current affairs than I have for years. I would even go so far as to say that Flipboard is one of the most compelling reasons for someone to buy a tablet as it can turn even the most news-phobic person into a keen reader. It also allows an element of interaction as often you can comment on the story or share it with your Twitter/Facebook connections as you read it.

So, if you have an iPhone/android phone or tablet I think you should give this app a try.

Pay per click (PPC) – where social and traditional marketing collide

I think it was probably Google that saw the old advertising model was broken ... at least in many people's eyes. The fundamental flaw in how all advertising works is that you pay before you get any benefit and, worse still, you pay because the salesperson tells you this will increase your sales/customer flow/awareness.

Previously it didn't matter if you advertised on TV, in the newspapers, on radio, in magazines, on billboards ... anywhere, you were charged based on the number of people who were exposed to your ad.

The most expensive billboard site in the UK is on the A4 in London, at the junction of Warwick Road (well, it always used to be the most expensive). Anyway, the reason it costs so much money to have a billboard here is because it's a very, very busy road. The busiest arterial road into London, in fact. Add to this that vehicles have to stop at the traffic lights here every minute and it really is a prime site. If 200,000 cars drive past every day and cars have an average of 1.2 occupants, clearly 240,000 people will be exposed to the advert.

If those people drive past to and from work 5 days every week that's 2,400,000 impressions (number of times the ad is viewed) and 10 impacts per week (the number of times each person is exposed to the ad).

However, as an advertiser you're taking a lot on faith.

- Many of these 240,000 people won't ever see the ads because they are driving along the road, not looking at the scenery.
- Even if a driver sees the ad he or she might not be interested in the product.
- The driver might be listening to the radio and make a connection between your brand and an unrelated product.
- The ads will be less visible when it's dark or raining.
- People may be in too much of a hurry to pay attention to the message.

Whatever the situation, we can pretty much guarantee that, if you're exposing your message to 240,000 people twice every day, you won't get 240,000 extra hits on your website. If you've not got the right ad you might get no additional traffic to your site.

With PPC, though, you pay by results. You agree to pay a certain cost (usually pence) for each click on one of your adverts. You can set an overall budget and absolutely know that you're only paying for results, like this.

- Bid price, the amount you're prepared to pay for a click (say 25p).
- Overall budget (say £10/day).

With PPC you know that if you are being charged £10/day, you are getting at least 40 visitors (possibly more if the price you end up paying is less than your maximum bid of 25p). For advertisers this is brilliant because they can base their budgets on how many visitors they need to get rather than how much media space costs. Also, unlike a Yellow Pages advert, it can be switched off at any point if no further enquiries are needed.

The first major player in this market was Google. The nature of a search is that you don't know anything about the searcher, but you know that, at the moment the search is conducted, the searcher is interested in 'pink fluffy slippers' (or whatever it is that is being searched for) and Google provides the results that it feels best match the search query.

As always with PPC, you pay only if someone actually clicks the link. This is great if you are selling a product that people know they need. If, however, you're selling a new product or trying to break into an existing market where there is a very strong leader or a generic term that happens to be a brand/product name of one of the other companies (such as 'Coke', 'Hoover' or 'Sellotape'), it becomes very difficult to gain any traction. In fact, sometimes you have to refer to your own product by a competitor's name. This is an inherent problem with using Google AdWords for some businesses.

However, the other side of that particular coin is Facebook PPC advertising. You know nothing about what the person you're advertising to is looking for (like every other type of advertising except Google AdWords), but you know far more about the person you're displaying the advert to than on pretty much any other platform.

With Facebook advertising you can see (in real time) how many of the total Facebook population in any given country you can talk to with your adverts by the following criteria:

- location (either town, city or radius from a given point)
- age
- sex
- interests
- connection level to you/your business page
- relationship status
- languages spoken
- level of education (e.g. secondary and degree)
- workplace.

As of January 2013 there were 32,600,000 people in the UK registered on Facebook (see Figure 17.1) – that represents just over 52 per cent of the entire population (and considerably more than 52 per cent if you discount the very ends of the age spectrum as they aren't present on Facebook). So this represents a fantastic resource for general marketing and real-time targeting analysis – for example, I know that today there are 243,240 female university graduates who are engaged to be married.

This sort of market insight is available to everyone for nothing whenever they want it and should be part of the planning of each and every business decision.

As far as Facebook advertising goes, it's great because it enables you to micro-niche your product or service to make the advert as compelling as possible because, like Google, part of the calculation regarding how much you actually pay per click is based on click-through rate (CTR), so there's a real incentive to make the advert compelling.

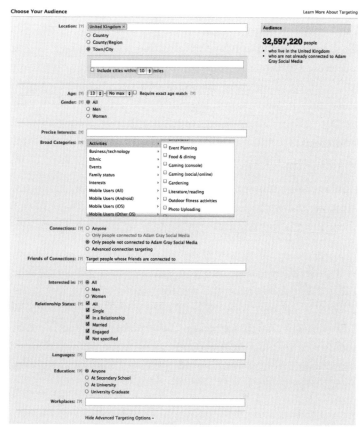

Figure 17.1 Facebook PPC audience analysis

To illustrate the point, imagine that you are an 18-year-old boy. One of the adverts in Figure 17.2 is significantly less appealing to you than the other one.

Figure 17.2 Facebook PPC ads

If you are targeting a broad demographic, then producing a series of ads reading, 'If you are 18 ...', 'If you are 19 ...', 'If you are 20 ...' is a much more effective way of talking to your audience. Certainly if I saw an ad that read 'Are you in your 40s, balding, interested in technology ... then click here' I would find it pretty much irresistible. As an advertiser it costs no more to run a campaign containing literally hundreds of ad variants, but finding the magic formula can have a dramatic effect on your CTR ... and therefore your costs.

This micro-niching makes your ads more effective, more cost-effective and more engaging. The only question you have is where the ads should direct traffic: to your Facebook page or to your website?

As a general rule of thumb you can probably expect a higher level of engagement if the people who click the link arrive at your Facebook page than if they arrive at your website. However, for tactical campaigns you might have specific functionality or transactional capabilities on your website that you simply can't get on your Facebook page. Sort of swings and roundabouts really.

 **recap**

- Think about how the different elements of your digital marketing can work together.

- PPC, search marketing, social media should all drive traffic not to your homepage but to the most appropriate page for the contact that you're discussing, this is vital to maximise results from what you're doing.

CHAPTER 18

Understanding and managing risks

Usually larger businesses tend to be more aware of risk than smaller businesses, but there are risks involved in using social media even if you have taken every reasonable security step that you can. Before looking at these risks, let's first say that you don't really have much choice any more about using social media: your clients are there, so you really need to be there too. Nevertheless, understanding what the risks and variables are is pretty important.

Risk number 1: your own team

People make mistakes. I know this sounds obvious, but it's true. People do things without thinking and then they repent at their leisure. The problem, obviously, with people saying or doing inappropriate things is that instead of being confined to the group of friends you were in a bar with, all of a sudden the problem can be presented to a global audience. So, you need to educate your staff and colleagues. They need to understand that, unlike when they're behind the counter or on the telephone dealing with customers, the amplification their message can be given is enormous.

To give you some idea of what can go wrong, one of the UK's bigger mobile phone companies dismissed a member of the marketing team, but before he left he was able to send just one last tweet ... at this point the company had just under 8,000 followers. His tweet was unpleasant but short enough that it could be retweeted with comments. Because it came from this large, well-regarded company it was retweeted, many times.

Although the tweet itself was deleted within a couple of minutes it was already in the public domain and was viewed by 750,000 people.

Of course, this was a mistake in as much as passwords weren't changed, but it goes to show how quickly messages can spread if they capture the imagination or are funny. It is vital that everyone in your company who uses social media understands this – even if they say things from their own accounts in their own time, if it's possible to tie their comments back to your company there's a good chance it will happen.

Risk number 2: vesting control

At least with your own staff you have a modicum of control. You can't guarantee that they won't do anything silly or make mistakes, but where comments and opinions can be aired by people who aren't under your control you really have no say whatsoever.

Even when you run a structured campaign and you think you've thought of everything, things can go wrong. Often this is because there's always a smart Alec who wants to score points. That's just human nature, but it isn't going to make it any easier.

For example, the supermarket chain Waitrose (which has a very loyal following) decided to launch the Twitter campaign 'I shop at Waitrose because ...'. Well, with hindsight you can see that it's asking for trouble, but I don't think Waitrose could have predicted the avalanche of funny comments that it triggered.

Some examples included, 'I shop at Waitrose because everyone on our estate does. Even the gamekeepers.' and 'I shop at Waitrose as it's the only place where my kids' tantrums are classed as splendidly Montessori, darling.'

Later Waitrose said how 'thrilled they were with the huge number of funny responses that the campaign had received'. Of course, there's the old adage 'there's no such thing as bad publicity' and the campaign certainly received more of that than Waitrose realistically could have hoped for, but taking this kind of sarcasm on the chin requires a certain sort of thick-skinned attitude and there are plenty of smaller, younger businesses which perhaps might not have weathered the storm in the way Waitrose managed to do.

Fairly regularly we see comments on social media taken out of context or misreported and then getting blown out of all proportion and it's important to understand that this is 'the nature of the beast'. There's nothing you can do to absolutely safeguard against this and while it could, theoretically, cause mayhem and perhaps even damage to your business, it seldom does ... and it's hardly ever long-lasting even if it does.

These problems come and go and a single incident, while it may seem dreadful at the time, will seldom in itself damage a relationship. However, you don't want bad things to happen too often because people's decisions are usually based on the sum of all the knowledge they have about you and your brand – 1,000 good things and 20 bad things mean you are probably a good person/company to be working with; 1,000 good things and 150 bad things ... not such a good bet. Clearly, minimising these potential situations is important, and for those that are outside your control, understanding how to deal with them in an effective and friendly manner is vital.

Some years ago British Airways carried out research on customer satisfaction and the results showed that customers who had had a problem or bad experience which had been dealt with effectively and to their satisfaction were seven times more likely to recommend BA to a friend. So sometimes a problem can be a good thing. If you talk about customer service and your ability to deal with problems, it's just words, but if you're able to really deliver to your customers during a crisis, you may well have created customers for life.

During autumn 2012, the UK's largest mobile phone operator, O2, suffered a major technical problem that meant millions of its customers were left with patchy or no service for hours and in some cases days. Social media channels were rife with jokes and complaints from the usually happy customers – although one would assume that the comments weren't posted from mobile devices! O2 responded quickly and with humour, prompting some positive tweets from customers including 'Whoever's running the @O2 Twitter account WINS at social media *tips hat*' and '@O2 I think I'm in love'.

This kind of engagement tends to come from teams that are comfortable talking in this space and are empowered to deal with the comments quickly and in the way they see fit. The normal way of dealing with situations like this is to answer comments that are important or you can put a good spin on and ignore militant or particularly abusive comments to avoid drawing attention to them and to stop further similar comments. However, O2 took the brave stance to answer every single comment, including the colourful ones.

Yes, the company had empowered its staff to compensate unhappy customers, but more importantly it had empowered them to be the human face of this problem. The interesting point about being human was that the negative comments and aggressive tirades gradually started to turn into support, such as '@O2 I still think you're great!!'. This is something we see fairly regularly in the social media world because people are interacting with brands in the same way and in the same places that they interact with their friends and people they admire.

This is great, but not uncommon. What was uncommon was how O2 managed to get people to stop talking about the problem and start talking about the good stuff: the accessible, human nature of O2 itself and the fact that it was actually listening to complaints.

O2 went further still by managing to use the ensuing conversations as a positive marketing tool. Yes, the company was dealing with a problem, but once again it humanised it and engaged followers in a cool and friendly way.

> the company was dealing with a problem, but once again it humanised it

Social media in the media

There are many books about internet security from all possible perspectives – technical, corporate, financial and personal. Most of the solutions are common sense, although there is a trend in books such as Andrew Keen's *The Cult of the Amateur* (Nicholas Brealey, 2008) suggesting that perhaps social media is an evil, unwholesome thing that is damaging to both individuals and societies as a whole or at best undermines the cultural pinnacles we have achieved. This discussion is large and outside the scope of this book, but while there are risks, of course, social media is here to stay and it is the landscape in which we operate, whether we like it or not.

Facebook is a personal network, LinkedIn is your personal CV, Twitter is your personal microblog. The more you promote yourself and grow your audience, the more you are presenting yourself to people who may not be all they seem. Tread carefully. Don't give out your personal details or telephone number to anyone before you've met them face to face and got to know them. Don't meet anyone alone or in an unfamiliar venue. In every society – towns, cities, countries and social networks – there are people who aren't nice and you need to be wary – not paranoid but wary. Just make sure you always take appropriate precautions with your online persona and you'll be fine.

Although annexed at the back of the book (and possibly, if you've got this far, this isn't relevant any more), often the biggest hurdle that people (and particularly businesses) have to overcome before really adopting social media is: fear.

Hardly a day goes past when there isn't something in the newspapers about 'the evil' of social media. People wasting their lives on Facebook, people unable to forge relationships in the real world, people losing their jobs through comments that they've made, the total erosion of moral values in society ... what a load of rubbish!

Social media is simply a mirror for our behaviours. People say silly things on Facebook in much the same way that they say silly things in a bar with their friends. The difference with social media is that now those poorly considered comments can be shared with a huge audience. In reality, though, that's always been the case: for generations people have been selling their stories to newspapers, exposés of people's deepest, darkest secrets have been the underpinning of the entire tabloid newspaper industry. The only difference now is that everyone is a journalist and the news media is free.

> now those poorly considered comments can be shared with a huge audience

The risks have always been there, it's just that these days there's a much greater possibility of your comments or actions coming back and biting you on the backside.

Personally I don't see Facebook and its relentless data mining, or Twitter and its ability to spread news so quickly, as bad things, they're just the landscape in which we now live. The news reports about how we've fallen out of love with Facebook hold little or no water because people are still signing up faster than they are leaving. Facebook continues to grow and whether you are a promoter of Facebook or a detractor, your ability to have a social life is increasingly being influenced by whether or not you are on the same social network as your friends. Of course, it doesn't mean that unless you connect with the right people means you will not ever get a dinner invitation, but it does mean you'll probably get fewer.

So, as I said earlier in the book, there's actually far more to potentially be gained than lost.

brilliant recap

- Whenever you release control of how your brand is portrayed in the marketplace you face the risk that the public might not treat it with the same reverence as you do.

- These days, however, your brand is there whether you like it or not.

- To manage this you must be prepared to meet criticism and sarcasm head on, in the same way that you would do in a face-to-face environment. If you do, you could possibly turn a negative situation into a huge positive.

CHAPTER 19

How to build social media into the rest of your marketing

Within any business there are differing marketing opportunities vying for marketing time and budget. I am not suggesting that any business should abandon its other (possibly very successful) marketing activities and throw itself into only social media in the short term, although I do think that within five years social media will be the biggest marketing, customer service and branding expenditure that any business has. However, in the short to medium term, social media needs to perfectly mesh with other marketing activities. It needs to prove its worth and demonstrate a better return on investment and higher levels of engagement than can be generated from more traditional marketing techniques.

A good starting point is to offer your various audiences the opportunity to connect with you on all of your platforms as they come online. Simple things like publishing your Facebook page address in all your advertising and your LinkedIn details on your email footers and business cards will help enormously with maximising cross-pollination between platforms.

> offer your various audiences the opportunity to connect with you on all of your platforms

Of course, this is not rocket science, but it is the sort of thing that is often overlooked in the rush to get the various platforms live. It's all very well launching on Facebook or Twitter, but initially, to get some traction, you're probably going to want to use some offline marketing to let people know that you're there. Adverts, posters, flyers, newsletters, letterheads, business cards, email, database, outdoor signage, car stickers, banners at exhibitions are all ways to let people know that they can contact you in loads of different places because, with so many people and businesses on these networks, it's very unlikely you're the only Angela Smith there. So, you need to tell people that you are there and where possible make sure you do it in such a way they can't mistype it or forget it.

Remember that some people would rather connect with your business on Facebook than they would subscribe to your newsletter. Some people would rather follow you on Twitter than they would on LinkedIn. If you want to maximise the penetration that your business has, you need to try to be where your clients and prospects want you to be, because, when you are, they are more likely to be sympathetic to your message.

One of the huge benefits of marketing online, in all its guises, is that you can start to link the different activities. It's simple to put a 'Like us on Facebook' link on your website or a 'Follow me on Twitter' link in the foot of your email; in fact, many of these things can be done easily by you or your team.

As is always the way with the social media space, though, you need to consider why someone would want to comment on or share what it is that you've posted. The reality is that as much as you'd like them to do it because they love you, they won't. What they need is an incentive. Now, when I say incentive I don't mean you need to actually incentivise them, simply that they must engage with the topic or the item. However, this linking can be so much more, from at one end of the scale simply having 'Log in with Facebook' functionality for parts of your website so you can start to personalise the experience and get some feedback from what happens on your site to visitors' social networks, to at the other end producing something as innovative as Levi's Friends Store, which offers amazing integration with Facebook so you can see how many people like which products and your friends can even give feedback as to which product they think you should buy.

Of course, Levi's has deep pockets and a team able to brainstorm and integrate such innovative ideas, but every business can learn from what organisations such as Levi's has done and find ways to leverage the social networks of their connections to help spread their message. It just requires a bit of thought as to what you're trying to achieve ... pretty much everything can be done, you just need to think about what your customers really need and want.

In March 2011 a new image-sharing site launched, Pinterest, and while it really didn't do that much differently from any of the plethora of other sites out there such as Flickr and Picassa, it somehow seemed to attract great photos of beautiful things. Shortly after this a funky new online retailer called Fab was founded. Well, not actually 'founded' as it had been around for about a year as a social network, but about this time it 'pivoted' what it did to become an online retailer with daily design inspirations. Fab sells lovely designer products across all price ranges and all verticals – the only thing that the products have in common is that they are all beautifully designed and beautifully photographed (a quick visit to **Fab.com** will show you what I mean).

Fab's founders are social media entrepreneurs and they recognised that the way to spread the word about the site quickly and effectively was through social media channels. So they built social media into their offering at the most fundamental level. At every opportunity they encourage you to sign in using Facebook rather than with an email address – you can't even place anything in your basket without signing in. Every single picture has a Facebook 'Like' button and a Pinterest 'Pin it' button next to it (see Figure 19.1). A simple 'click' against any product you like the look of will share it across the most design-focused of the image-sharing sites and the largest social network of all … driving more recognition and more visits back to the **Fab.com** site.

Figure 19.1 How Fab integrates Facebook and Pinterest

Clearly this strategy is pretty successful – at the beginning of 2012 Fab had 100 staff and 2,000 product lines; by the end of the year it had 600 employees and 14,000 products. In November 2011, five months after relaunching, Fab had 1 million members, reaching this number faster than Facebook, Twitter and even Groupon. In September 2012 it had 7.5 million members, then in December that year it passed the 10 million mark.

On the back of this hunger to make the shopping experience more beautiful and more integrated with social media, Fab has launched iPhone and iPad apps and you can be pretty sure there will be more to follow. This success is, I'm sure Fab would agree, largely down to how it has been able to integrate social media and commerce in a beautiful and user-friendly package.

The key thing is to try to understand what you can learn for your business from organisations like Fab. I don't mean copy what they do (although if you need a starting point there are worse places), but understand how your business might be able to harness the power of social sharing to grow in the way Fab has. Remember, the key learning here is to innovate: the first past the post is the winner and there's no silver medal for coming second.

> understand how your business might be able to harness the power of social sharing

Now, you might at this point be saying 'I don't want to have 10 million customers' or 'I want to remain small but be more profitable'. Social media is about providing recognition and, from that, options. If you have three times as many enquiries, you don't need to accept all of them. You can be choosier about who you work with. You can raise your prices. You can make the choice about which regions and industries you prefer. Having a surplus of work means that you have choice. Creating the surplus can be a function of your reputation. Your reputation can largely be down to social media.

> you can be choosier about who you work with

You need to remember that, while social media can be great fun, educational and enlightening, from a business perspective you're using it primarily as a marketing tool. You are using it as a channel for your business to interact with your customers and as such it needs to be treated as part of the structure of the business.

brilliant recap

- Social media can offer huge marketing benefits for an organisation, but, for best effect, it needs to form part of a coherent marketing strategy.

- Adding social media links to your business cards, your website and your emails is a great start, but understanding the customers' buying journeys is crucial and recognising that, like any chain or process, it's only as good as its weakest link.

- If your website doesn't convert many of the visitors into customers, then driving more visitors there through your social media (even if they do already like you as a result of it) probably isn't going to yield the results that you want.

Conclusion

Social media is here to stay. Every business is going to need a well-structured, well-thought-through presence in the future in order to be competitive. Fact.

As people migrate more and more from old media and communication ideas to new, interactive, real-time media, businesses need new strategies to capitalise on these opportunities.

Too often, though, businesses regard social media as a solution for their sales department or their email system rather than seeing it as an holistic solution for engaging with their customers. Social media isn't about forcing your messages down the throats of your customers – that's the old way. Terms such as 'impacts', 'penetration' and 'share of voice' are both outdated and an inherently invasive way of considering your customers. Social media is about building relationships, about making friends, about winning confidence and then letting the business come to you.

To implement this kind of strategy requires thought, patience and a deep-rooted belief that getting closer to your customers is the way forward for your business. Yes, there are businesses that have focused their communications around social media and many of them are doing incredibly well, but you don't have to do this ... yet.

What you do need to do, though, and do quickly, is to develop a social presence and have a plan for how your business can interact with its customers in the social space. This is straight-forward and requires no magic or even any great creativity, but it does require a little bit of thought and commitment.

✖ brilliant checklist

1 Understand what social media is and how your business can adopt conversations in a positive way.
2 Identify someone internally who can ensure that it happens.
3 Learn the basics of social media and develop a plan.
4 Agree a timescale internally for this to happen.
5 Work out how this fits in with the rest of your marketing.
6 Prioritise a list of the platforms you want to be on.
7 Create the social presence.
8 Train the members of staff who are going to use social media.
9 Measure your results and hone your presence.

If you follow the steps in the checklist, gradually creating your presence on each of the platforms, then connecting and engaging with your customers and prospects, then measuring and refining what you do, you simply cannot fail.

Almost every business recognises that time spent networking is valuable to the business. Social media allows you to network with as many people as you want to, efficiently and when both you and they want to, so bear in mind that 'playing' on many of these networks is in fact working, in exactly the same way as going to a networking event and just 'chatting' is working because it's sharing your expertise and reinforcing that you are a good business.

> time spent networking is valuable to the business

The basic principles of being courteous, helpful, knowledge-able and generally to nice people will serve you very well in the world of social media.

Note on general good practice

Well, this should all be pretty straightforward. You need to be charming, you need to be patient and you need to recognise that everything you say can be re-shared, irrespective of your personal security settings, so you should really consider whether or not the comment that you're going to make could be damaging if taken out of context.

The key thing to remember is that, unless you're Ashton Kutcher or Stephen Fry, people aren't actually waiting for you to say something, they're too busy getting on with their lives. So you need to be consistently good and demonstrate you always add value to your followers and trust that eventually things will work out all right in the social media space … because they probably will.

Glossary

+1 the Google+ equivalent of a Facebook 'like'.

Analytics a free Google code that, when placed on your website, gives insights into visitors' behaviour, such as how many pages they've visited, how long they've spent and their journey through the site.

App short for application. Can run either within one of the social networks (such as Facebook or LinkedIn) or on your phone/tablet.

Bit.ly a URL shortener.

Direct message a non-public communication within a social network, usually between two people who follow each other. This is the social media equivalent of sending someone an email.

Facebook the world's largest network – more than 1 billion members on two types of pages, personal and business. Supported by mobile apps for most devices. Many plugins, games and apps available. Regarded as not just the largest but also one of the 'stickiest' sites there is, with an average of one in eight online minutes being spent on Facebook.

Fans now referred to as 'likes', these are people who have registered with your Facebook Business Page as a subscriber. They receive a notification every time something is added to your 'wall'. The number of these likes/fans is the number of people who will directly receive your updates (although this doesn't mean that they will necessarily see or read them, of course).

Flipboard a smartphone/tablet application that aggregates content for your social networks in a newspaper-type format.

Follower the term for someone who has subscribed to your updates on Twitter/LinkedIn/YouTube. In the case of LinkedIn, someone can become a follower (subscribe to your updates) without becoming a connection.

Google Plus/Google+ Google's social network, rather like a cross between Facebook and Twitter.

Hashtag a Twitter term for a label that is applied to a tweet to indicate it is about a specific topic to make it easier to find.

HootSuite a social media management tool that offers very good reporting.

Instagram a photo app for mobiles. It allows you to take photos, add an effect (such as sepia), frame them and then share them on Instagram, Facebook, Twitter, Flickr, Foursquare and Tumblr. It's a great little app and can be cool to use some of the time for giving your photos a bit of visual interest. Now owned by Facebook.

Keyword a word or phrase for that you want to be found (in my case it might be 'social media expert').

Likes *see* Fans.

LinkedIn the largest business-focused online network. People can meet, share ideas and expertise and conduct business. There were 200 million members as at January 2013.

Log-in the process of confirming your identity to access one of your accounts.

Mention when somebody talks to their network but references your username (exposing you to a potentially new market).

Monitoring listening to what is being said about you in the social media space.

Ow.ly a URL shortener owned by HootSuite.

Poke a Facebook hangover from the early days, like a digital nod to someone – it doesn't do anything other than just remind them that you're still there. It tends to be used far less than it was. However, Mark Zuckerberg, one of the co-founders of Facebook, has just written a 'poke' app for the iPhone, so it may be coming back into fashion.

Post usually on Facebook Business Pages or Google+, tends to be a more substantial article than a simple status update. Could be text, images, a link or even a video clip.

PPC stands for pay per click, an advertising term denoting a new sort of advertising where you pay for the people who respond to your advert rather than for placing it. Much higher accountability and lower risk for the advertiser.

Retweet peculiar to Twitter, where one of your followers shares a tweet of yours to their followers (thus exposing you to potentially new contacts).

ROI return on investment, the measure of whether or not your social media (or anything else) is profitable for the business.

Sentiment is what's being said about you, good or bad.

Share where you promote a comment, link, photo, etc. to your network.

Sign-up the process of joining a social network. Invariably free, usually requires an email address (for confirmation), then allows you to add contact details and often a photo too.

Sprout Social a social media management tool that offers very good reporting.

Status update the way that you share information with your network – something you've read, what you're doing, general news, etc.

Subscriber someone who registers for updates (typically on your blog).

Tag a label applied to a blog post, a photo or a video that helps people to find it when searching for key topics, etc. it might contain.

Tagged when your name is added to another person's tweet in which you appear which you appear or you are identified in a Facebook, Google+ or LinkedIn post or photograph.

Timeline the way that most social sites like to display chronologically important information, such as what's going on within your network. Generally the older things will be at the bottom and the newer things will be at the top.

Tweet the term for the 140-character updates that people share on Twitter.

Twitter a 500 million-strong network where you can share short stories and pieces of information of 140 characters or fewer. Good for breaking news and seeing what's going on in the world right now.

Username your unique title/name within a social network (try to get the same username across as many networks as possible). On Twitter, your username is denoted by having an @ before it.

Vanity URL shortener it is now possible to have your own personalised URL shortener, such as goo.gl (Google), Link.in (LinkedIn), fb.me (Facebook), vir.gn (Virgin), etc.

Wall your Facebook page (now often referred to as your timeline because of its chronological nature) where everything that you've said or people have said to you publicly will be visible to a visitor.

YouTube part of the Google empire and the world's largest video-sharing site. Video clips hosted here can be placed within other web pages (such as your own website), saving both bandwidth and hosting space. YouTube is also the world's second-largest search engine (after Google). Half a billion members as at the start of 2013.

Index